THE
ORACLE
BOOK

Robert Alan–Haven

First published in Great Britain in 2011 by

Bannister Publications Ltd
118 Saltergate
Chesterfield
Derbyshire S40 1NG

Typeset in Palatino Linotype by Escritor Design.
Cover design by The Design Kabin, Chesterfield, Derbyshire

Printed and bound in the UK by the MPG Books Group
Bodmin and King's Lynn

Robert Alan-Haven

The deep interplay between the subjective and objective worlds manifest in the human condition has formed the focus of Robert's life. Profound empirical learning is the basis of his work together with the ability to make the intangible tangible in words.

The drive to unlock the psychological and spiritual realities behind all things has been ever–present and fruitful in the unfolding of his conscious attention to personal process.

He has been a healer, massage therapist, psychotherapist, rebirther, personal development group leader, speaker, writer, dolphinswim group organiser, holistic practitioner, astrologer, and presentation skills trainer.

Acknowledgements

I would like to acknowledge a small number of special people. For their encouragement and positive responses during the long time of testing the content of this book in their own lives, I would like to thank **Teresa-Iche, Maria Kavallierou, Gerry Pead** and **Jon Mason**. Their contributions to me personally and to the nurturing of the original concept have been immeasurable.

My sincere thanks are due also to **Audrey Williams** for her vital contribution to the production of this book.

INTRODUCTION

We all have times when some form of guidance, advice, or wise counsel, would be most welcome. Sometimes we actively seek it, sometimes it comes unbidden before we even realise we need it. It has been said that the universe will give us what we need before it gives us what we want, and the ways this can come into the form of our lives are legion.

In common with so many others, I have experienced those moments when a phrase or a simple sentence has leapt off the pages of a book I have been reading and the words have resonated with my state of being at the time. Similar 'eureka' moments have arisen from everyday conversations, and from innumerable media sources. Equally, there have been many times when I have deliberately opened a book at random, sometimes with a specific question in my head, sometimes not, to find an appropriate revelation in the words of the page before me.

Inspiration has played a part too, in the sense that, just as randomly, relevant words and phrases, even the words of songs(!), have appeared in my mind complete in themselves as an appropriate message, reminder, whatever, without any previous thought or rational process producing them. I have learned to trust such entries into my consciousness. Some of those have been included amongst the wisdom of others herein.

This book is my attempt to bring together these forms of such apparently random guidance, together with those maxims that have been the most helpful to me over the years, and make conscious use of them in the pages that follow.

HOW TO USE THIS BOOK

Like everything else in the physical universe the pages here will get in line with what is present in your energy system beneath the surface waiting to be recognised. Often they will be reminders of a familiar principle working in your life which has temporarily passed from your conscious mind. Sometimes they will bully you into submission! During a time of persistent longing to be living in another culture, another land, I was faced repeatedly with the quote *They change their climate, not their lives, who rush across the sea* until I got the message and let go the attachment I had to being somewhere else as a means of improving my life.

As the supporting texts reveal, there is so much to be gleaned from each saying that simply opening at any one of them can provide a wealth of guidance. I have found that whatever I do prior to making my choice, what I am presented with is always appropriate, showing me what I most need to hear in the moment. If you prefer to use a specific routine of preparation of your own state of mind and emotions before a choice is made then, again, that is up to you. The apparent random nature of the exercise doesn't alter the basic truth that the lesser has no choice but to reflect the greater.

The human element can be just yourself or a group setting. Each and every text has such potential for prompting self examination, thoughts, feelings, inspiration, that sharing what comes up in response to the content can be the basis for anything from a brief discussion to a weekend workshop!

There will be times when you have neither the time nor the inclination to go deeply into the supporting text, and yet you need clarification. Then it may be helpful to go to a second page to give clues as to how the message in the original page is operating. As an example, let's say your first choice is *Argue for your limitations and you get to keep them*, and you might think 'Do I? If so, why do I do that?' So, opening at a second page, up comes *Your fears are unable to exist in the same space where love and gentleness abide*. What you may get from that is that your fear in your current situation prevents you from going beyond your existing boundaries, so you argue for them as the safest course.

It is my belief that there is no such thing as an accident or coincidence. Opening this book where you may will always have something for you. The texts in support of each aphorism are wide ranging, from the practical to the spiritual, via the emotional and psychological, so don't expect any complete text to be wholly relevant.

Bear in mind that the words are like variations on a theme. The basic melody is in the heading and is the essence of what is required. To back that up, the texts provide colour, clarification, light and shade so that, occasionally, some of what any one of them contains will be in the foreground of your perception and demand focus, whilst the rest of that particular text may remain as simply interesting comment, for that moment. In other words there will be times when parts of the texts leap off the page at you – fine – be selective, discriminate, take note, the next time you open at that page there may be a different facet of the same energy to follow.

Give your past to God, and your future too, and pray for the wisdom to live them both as they arise

If the word 'God' doesn't do it for you, then please substitute your own symbolic vocabulary for the ultimate omnipresent Divinity. However you choose to identify the unidentifiable, this is about another variation on the theme of surrender.

Unless our awareness is totally focused in the moment, through a meditative process or an intense physical activity, our thoughts will usually be dominated by the past or the future. The events, thoughts, feelings rooted in the past are continually rehashed – what was, what could have been, what should have been. Concerns, worries, fears on the one hand, together with expectations, hopes, plans on the other, take our thoughts into the future.

Of themselves these mental processes are neither right nor wrong, they simply are that way, there is no point in judging yourself for having them work like that – it would be like remonstrating with a tape recorder for being a tape recorder! All that is happening is that survival mind is doing what it is programmed to do, which is to take you away from now, the present moment, where transformation awaits, and putting your attention continually into the past or the future, thereby keeping you 'in your head'.

Mystical traditions of ancient Eastern religions liken the conditioned mind to the chatterings of an insane monkey! The problems arise when we identify with the chatterings, when we are sucked in to the rantings as if they constitute the sum total of who we are. You may find yourself in this position, and therefore carrying a heavy load of mental and emotional baggage around attached to your past and your future.

The time is ripe for you to give it away, to surrender it to Divine Intelligence, Great Spirit, God, the Oneness beyond duality, however you perceive It. Acknowledge that you can't handle the burdens of attachment to your past and your future, the weight is too much, and hand them over to a Power that can, and always will, given the chance.

The promise is that you won't lose anything at the mundane level which is really important for you to experience. You will do whatever you have to do regardless of the temporal origins of the doing. The point is you will be going through the motions of doing in a surrendered state, and that is what transforms the burden.

Heaven and hell are internal states of being. Be prepared to pray, to ask for the ability to recognise what's going on and the wisdom of this maxim will come to you, the ability to surrender to the existence of your past and your future as being only concepts compared to the empirical reality of now. Be present; give the rest away.

Life is not personal.
The life expanded is transpersonal

If you have chosen this text you are probably going through a personal crisis of some sort. Time to bear in mind that the only constant in life is change. Everyone has personal crises at one time or another – home, family, relationship, career, money, health, and on and on. The common ones, the stuff of life, are normally related to outer circumstances. That is not to say the inner life does not alter during or after the outer change, there may have been a change of attitude, or what felt like some aspect of so called personal growth, but cause is normally attached to the outer compulsions.

This time it's different. There is a realisation that you have been through similar scenarios before. The form may have changed, the people involved are not the same, the props are different if you like, but your feelings, thoughts, reactions are familiar, uncomfortably so. The script may appear to change, but your role remains essentially the same.

There are two possibilities. You may be moving from a state of victimhood to personal responsibility, realising from the continual repetition of certain crises, and your reactions to them, that you are contributing something central to the process. If that is the case, then congratulations are in order, because that move out of being a victim is a huge step toward your liberation and an expanded quality of life.

On the other hand you could be close to despair because not only have you accepted personal responsibility, but, having done so, you have been 'working on yourself' for some time, and yet here you are again in a place which is all too familiar. If this is where you find yourself then the message of this text is profound. It is a reminder that coming from the machinery, the structure of the personal, when attempting to 'grow' – which normally means trying to release some part of you which still feels 'wrong' – cannot succeed.

In the first place there is a blueprint for that structure which has been in place from your earliest moments, some would say even before that, and the blueprint can't redraw itself. Put another way it's like expecting a sound or video recording to change itself without input from another source. That other source is our expanded self, the transpersonal, i.e. that which transcends the personal. In a sense it is the unknown and the unknowable sea in which we all swim. The ocean of the Beloved if you like.

From that place you can observe your own persona and know that it is what it is, there's nothing wrong, there's nothing to change, there's nothing to work at, there's nothing to do. The lily doesn't spend its life trying to be a rose, an oak tree doesn't spend its life berating itself for not being a weeping willow – you get the point. Give up! Let go the struggle to be something or someone other than what and who you are. You are not here to comply with the 'oughts' and 'shoulds' of others.

Whatever is going on, be assured it is all in the grand scheme of things. There is always a desire to 'fix' the personal where gratification can only ever be temporary. There is everlasting satisfaction in the transpersonal, where nothing ever needs fixing!

Argue for your limitations and you get to keep them

The whole idea of this text is to make you aware just how much you limit yourself with thought and word, often unconsciously. You may be going through a time of opportunity in one or more areas of your life. If that is true, you are presented with a choice, which is to take the opportunity or refuse it. You have a part to play. If you are sufficiently free of compulsive reaction to make a true choice one way or the other, fine.

However, opening the book here suggests that that freedom does not exist in you at this time, which means that the apparent choice you may make is no choice at all but governed by your traditional, conditioned, probably negative, survival structures, in other words, you're on automatic pilot. Not only that, you'll back it up with a good rationale – lots of good reasons why you should stay exactly where you are. Now you're really arguing for your limitations, giving them lots of energy, cementing them in place.

However, life is always inviting us to expand our existing boundaries, which basically means saying 'yes' to the unknown. For some of us that can be a knee jerk reaction too, that can be just as automatic and choiceless as the negatives which govern the majority. If you are one of those then you could be unbounded and looking for the establishment of boundaries – for you choosing to say 'no' to some of the tempting new experiences which come your way would be just as fulfilling as a choice to say 'yes' to them would be for most of us. Paradoxical isn't it!

In the event, this page shows that you are more likely to be one of the majority of us who limit ourselves, day in and day out, by any number of automatic reactions which have one thing in common – they're all based on fear. Arguing for their validity normally starts with language like 'I can't', 'I couldn't possibly', 'I don't', 'I wouldn't', 'I won't', 'I shouldn't', 'I'm not', and similar. Let's be clear. There's nothing intrinsically wrong with negative responses. It is simply a time to be aware of where they come from, and if they are true, free choices on your part, or out dated and obsolete reactions from your past producing familiar avoidance and/or retreat.

Here's a way of checking the freedom, or otherwise, of your choices. Let's say a simple everyday proposal of a given course of action has been made to you, and out comes 'I can't'. Then that is challenged by the proposer, and your reaction becomes 'I can't because ....'

Now, get the proposer, if they are willing and able to of course, or, if not, someone who is when you are next in their company, to simply hear your reason without trying to answer it. Then they must ask you for another reason why you can't, and the next one, and so on. If you both can stay with that process until you run out of reasons, you may find yourself in a space within yourself where you can make a true choice which becomes either 'I can and I will' or 'I choose not to'.

Now you're not arguing for your limitations anymore, you are choosing where they are to be drawn, and you are empowered as a result.

Your fears can not exist where love and gentleness abide

One of the rules of the time and space system in which we live is that two objects cannot occupy the same space at the same time. This is equally true of the duality within us all. Heaven and hell, angels and demons, God (Old Testament depiction) and the Devil, are all representations, symbols of the two greatest causative drives in dualistic life as we live it, namely fear and love.

With a reasonable dose of self–awareness, at any one time our actions, thoughts, feelings in the moment can be traced back to being motivated by one or the other. Unless or until you are an avatar walking around in the oneness beyond duality, in the love that 'passeth all understanding', playing the game in this reality means experiencing the interplay between fear and love (as we know it) most of the time.

This page is a reminder to you to let in some love to that place within which is currently occupied by fear. A prayer from the Judaic tradition has it that 'The God of Fear and the God of Love are One. In the midst of action, making a tough decision, or in the contemplation of either, fear can dominate through our attachment to projected consequences, justified or not. The irrational can jump up and bite us on the backside, and then hang on like a terrier.

The trouble is that fear advertises its presence in many different ways – the way we look, what we say and how we say it, body language, in the energy system which reaches beyond the physical body. The result is that we can attract the very object of our fears because, in one sense, it already exists in us, held in place by the tentacles of fear.

It is time to let in another energy. Let that fearful space within you be taken over by love, in whatever form it takes to be acceptable to that ever present taskmaster in your head. Be gentle with yourself for a change, that will let in some love. The compassion you are capable of feeling for others – feel some of it for yourself, that will let in some love. Forgive yourself for being human enough to have the fear in the first place, that will let in some love.

As you do these things, these words will grow from a pleasant intellectual concept to become a deep personal experience you can draw on again and again. That process can be facilitated by a form of meditation. Putting all your attention on the breath, draw in life force on the in-breath from the very air around you to a point in the centre of the heart, then let the love and gentleness that will engender flow through you on the out-breath and fill every part of you like liquid gold – visualise that happening as you breathe.

The whole thing is an exercise in receiving, and whenever fear motivated thoughts come in, as they will, go back to the breath and take in that which is always available to you on a subtle level awaiting your invitation to enter.

There are parts of your humanity which can only be experienced in community, in relationship to others

Have you been hiding yourself away lately? Gone into retreat, into seclusion? Treading the lonely road? There are times in every life when these approaches are entirely appropriate. However, this text indicates that this is not the way for you right now. Reaching out to others, or another, is what is called for to answer needs which are surfacing in you. It may be a process which feels uncomfortable, even threatening sometimes, but taking the apparent risks involved can bring dividends at many levels of your existence. Much more than satisfying a hunger or scratching an itch.

Divine Oneness knew what it was doing when it created the illusion of separation. At the super conscious level the game is to see past the script, the roles, the scenarios and know that the self doesn't exist, cannot exist outside the Self in all its glory. For most of us sleepwalkers who occasionally have waking moments, the manifestation of unity lies in the pull of those needs which can only be fulfilled with the apparent other or others.

You may have a creative talent which you have been practising and keeping the results under wraps. You may have abilities in writing, drawing, painting, sculpting, cooking, music, the performing arts, creative play, making beautiful clothes, in fact making beautiful anything. Creativity is making something from nothing. The point is, if this applies to you, now is the time to reveal the products of your talent and risk the reactions of others, you might be surprised.

Communicate. Talk, write. Pick up the telephone, get on the internet, start conversations, make comment when you might normally keep your mouth shut. Reach out. Find ways of expressing affection or genuine regard when that is your truth. Pay compliments as a sincere gift, not as manipulation. Express appreciation of the talents of others. And don't forget the other part of communication, sometimes the gift of listening is such a balm to those who believe they are not heard.

What about touch? There's an oft neglected area. You need to share that with someone else to feel the real benefit. Sex too. You can hardly do that by yourself, well, you can create some of the sensations, but they are a pale reflection of the real thing. If they are as good as, or better than, joining with another, that may be precisely why this text is appropriate – it's time to investigate that further!

Finally, there is fulfilment in finding ways to contribute your energy to others. There is a deep need in all of us to feel we are contributing, again, one of those reflections of Oneness asserting itself. It could be random acts of kindness to complete strangers, or helping out someone near and dear, contributing to friends, or a group, or joining with others in a common cause which will contribute to society at large. Whatever you find to do, you will feel better about yourself, about belonging, about life, when you know you've done something which helps out, large or small. This is a time for altruism without personal agenda.

This sounds like a charter for a do-gooder, a busybody, so remember the essential balance you can offer is to receive. Being in relationship, in community, also means being able to receive when others want to feel the satisfaction in contributing to you.

It is often the smallest, most anonymous acts which create the loudest thunder in the spiritual world

You may be beating yourself up because you're not meditating every day, or you haven't set up a healing centre or sanctuary, or you're not out there teaching, passing on what you know. You may be just surviving from day to day when there is a drive, an expectation of yourself to be on the 'spiritual path'.

If you have turned to this text, the message is clear. It's *all* spiritual, so whatever you do registers in your energy field and therefore in the energy field of the whole planet. Every act sets up a vibration, and the quality of that vibration does not depend on magnitude or personal attachment.

We think we know what is important and what isn't. We think we know what makes a difference and what doesn't. In a word, we think we're in control. From that place we tend to measure what we do against some impossible scale of so called spirituality, and invariably appear to be left wanting, judged and sentenced by our own internal terminator!

Our conditioning to achieve carries over into our higher yearnings and demands great things. This text is a reminder that now is a time you can be content with what appear to be much lesser acts. Apparently it takes huge earth moving machines and explosives to move mountains. The greatest teacher of all told us that sometimes it takes no more than a mustard seed.

There is another place within us which is not interested in measuring or judging, or trying to determine whether or not an action will advance our growth or our spirituality. That place is centred in the heart and it is possible to recognise the difference by the spontaneity and feeling which arises with the action before rational thought takes a hold. See how easily they make their presence felt in response to the smallest act. That's what this text is about.

It is so easy to get sucked into the form of the action, and to want it to be attributable to us, to be recognised in some way for what we've done – understandable and very human (don't judge yourself for that either). Many great and worthwhile things are created which are tinged with desire and survival for the self – so what! 'By their deeds ye shall know them'.

The point of this text is that it's what is in the heart that matters when any act of service, great or small, is carried out. A random act of kindness, without thought of self, has the clarity and penetration of Cupid's arrow, it goes from the individual heart and adds immeasurably to the collective heart. This is a time for you to be aware that there are opportunities for you in the ordinary, the everyday, to create the most *extra*ordinary thunderstorms!

Words without actions are the assassins of idealism

This one hardly needs amplification. The words speak for themselves, and paradoxically, the meaning for you in choosing this text, is that the time for words alone is over.

It is likely that you have had an idea, which became an ideal, a dream about which you have become idealistic. It could be about your ideal life, the ideal relationship, your ideal career, your ideal home. It may have moved beyond the personal to the universal, in other words, you have seen a way ahead which would benefit society as a whole, or your local community, or a particular section of human or other organic life you see as deprived or threatened – the possibilities are endless.

Whatever it is, conception of the project has taken place. Following that, the next step into form inevitably involves words. The thoughts become articulate and are spoken, written, as the embryonic project takes shape. You may have talked about it with those nearest and dearest to you, the folks, if any, you can trust to give you honest feedback. Even as you have shared your ideas, there has been refinement in your thinking around them and how they would work in practice.

Alternatively, you may have kept the whole thing to yourself, discussing it within, writing everything down, adjusting, amending, developing. Either way, your idealism has become a world of words. Up to now that has been appropriate and necessary to the growth of the projected goal. The embryo has become a foetus approaching full term. It is time to act.

Opening the book here is a sure sign that, if the object of

your idealism is not to be stillborn, to give it birth in the world, you have to make your move, and you have to start the process now. Remember, as Thomas Jefferson said, 'One man with courage is a majority'. There may be fear, resistance, lots of 'oughts' and 'shoulds' in other directions, risks may have to be taken, and, with any or all of the above, do it anyway!

It may also be true for you that you don't have a massive, idealistic, life changing project in mind just now. This energy can apply equally to the mundane, the everyday, in that it is time for you to walk your talk in some way – to do what you have said you will do. That is the stuff of integrity and also worthy of being on this page.

Know that your very being is creative, everything springs from that, and that creativity is limitless. Expressing your creativity goes hand in hand with liberation, with transformation. As your idealism, at whatever level, comes into form it is literally trans-forming of your life, within and without.

The prize is worth it, and you are worthy of it. The words have done their job, now take what they have helped to form into the world. The Tao, in proper order, is Be – Do – Have. Being has made its presence felt through the vehicle of your creativity; now it is time for the doing.

The day thou gavest Lord is ended. The darkness falls at thy behest

The traditional religious language here might lead you to question its relevance to your present situation. Don't be misled however for the energy represented here is powerful.

Life is a process of change, indeed it has been said that the only constant in life is change. At one level, these words from a hymn at Evensong, simply acknowledge the inevitability of night following day, and that both are gifts from a power far beyond our control. There is no judgement here. In this context the light of day is not better than the darkness of night, or vice versa, it is simply that both are necessary to the full expression of life on this planet, and both have their contribution to make on the individual and the universal level.

This text is an indicator of inevitable change in your life. On a personal level you are at the dusk of a situation, a state of affairs, which has, literally, had its day. The sun is going down so you might as well enjoy the sunset, because there's nothing you can do to stop it. It may be a relationship, a friendship, a business or phase of your working life, a family matter, a death, a move to new climes. Perhaps a period of study has come to an end and it is time to practise your learning and your skills in the world. These are all typical outer manifestations of the interface represented here.

Inwardly there may be a sense that nothing will ever be the same again. It may even be the turning point which comes to us all sooner or later, namely the realisation that inner peace and satisfaction can never be made permanent residents through the attempted manipulation and control of outer conditions. Indeed, there is no permanence in any outer condition. The carousel of creation, preservation, and destruction continues with or without human participation. Every good story has a beginning, a middle, and an ending, and there is an ending presenting itself in your life which will not be denied. Resisting it will not serve you well.

Part of the lyric of a song from the wonderful musical 'Kiss Me Kate' sums up this energy. 'Where is the life that late I led? Where is it now? Totally dead!' Don't hang on. There is an aspect of your life; could be a person, a thing, a situation, an activity, an attitude, a behaviour pattern, a way of dealing with life inwardly or outwardly, which must be allowed to pass. Whatever it is, it has served its purpose. Let it go. The apparent darkness of the night to follow may feel threatening at first, but be assured, the night brings its own rewards.

One with courage is a majority

The history of human innovation, invention, discovery, exploration, is peopled with men and women who have manifested the energy of this page. The pioneers who move into unknown territory at any level are sometimes supported from the start of their venture, and subsequently idolised, that is if the area of expansion they choose is not perceived as a threat to the status quo.

The first lone sailor to circumnavigate the globe, the first man on the moon would perhaps belong in this category. However, for the most part, those who have brought breakthroughs which have led to life as we live it, from basic human rights issues to advances in travel, communications, mass entertainment and so on, have had to plough a lonely furrow through a mass of resistance, rejection and hostility before their ideas, inventions and discoveries saw the light of day and acceptance.

Moving from the universal to the personal, the meaning does not alter. Day in and day out life presents challenges which are personal and up close. What is risky and threatening to one may be a matter of ease to another. Opening the book here shows that you are in a situation which challenges you to respond with courage. You may be encountering resistance, negativity in one form or another, to an idea, a project, a proposal of some kind.

Whatever it is it represents to you the opportunity to expand, to venture into unknown territory within or without. It could be as simple as speaking your truth when you know you have been avoiding doing so. It is time to take a stand.

Another representation of this energy is to see it as a time to move out of your comfort zone in some aspect of your life. It may be that you have reached a point where the paradigms are set and to live within them is easy and comfortable. Only now it is too easy. Another part of you is demanding attention. It is time for a prison break – could be in a big way, or an apparently insignificant way, but it is significant to you, and that is what matters.

This is not a time to concern yourself with consequences, or approval, those matters are out of your hands. You may well feel totally alone in your convictions, yet whatever the world seems to be saying to you, stick with them, they are sound, otherwise you wouldn't be reading these words.

Look at the word courage. It contains 'rage', and that might help. You can tap into the energy of rage which lends itself to your commitment to the direction you want to take. Doesn't mean you have to act it out, it's simply that there is a huge reservoir of energy available in rage, and therefore in courage, to go your own way regardless. It can give you strength you never knew you had, and the timing is perfect for you to go 'where angels fear to tread'.

Let each period of wakefulness be accompanied by spiritual and physical exercise

You may be thinking that this is not particularly profound advice. Isn't this the kind of thing we are constantly being urged to do, or urging ourselves to do? That's probably true, however the value is in the timing. As is always the case with any kind of divination system, the fact that you have opened the book here at this time is no accident.

You may have been through a period of wondering why you don't feel better about yourself and about life after all you have done. You may have come a long way mentally and emotionally. You may have enlightened parts of your life in the sense that you've learned some lessons, applied them and seen some results. On the other hand, you may be at the beginning of your quest for greater awareness. Whatever has brought you to this point, it is time to attend to some simple everyday practices which can open the doors to a greater sense of well being.

Being human is to be part of an energy system which exists at many different levels simultaneously. Being able to move around within that system fluidly, easily, depending on the needs of the moment, is what keeps us in optimum health and well being.

Think of lock gates on a canal system. They are necessary to the maintenance of differing levels of water and to the safe and easy transition of boats between levels. If those gates fall into disrepair or are unused for too long, the whole system suffers. Perhaps some of your checks and balances are in need of what exercise can give them.

What's required here is a dose of self discipline, but it doesn't have to be the harsh domain of the internal taskmaster – you don't have to be hard on yourself to bring some discipline into your self expression. Think of it more as a gift you are giving to yourself, and that will become easier the more you feel the results.

I am not going to attempt to delineate what constitutes appropriate physical exercise for you. In this context it simply means get into your body, let the physical express itself. You will know what works for you better than anyone, or rather your body will – listen to it – and let it tell you when enough is enough. Divine Intelligence knew what it was doing when it clothed our bodies in muscle tissue, using it more than you have been doing will keep one of the essential lock gates in good order.

As to the spiritual exercise, that can take many forms as well. Prayer and meditation are generic terms and cover a multitude of approaches and methods. Visualisation, chanting, mantras, absent or distant healing, and on and on. Again what works for you is paramount rather than what anyone else says you 'should' do, so long as it is a part of your day spent attending to the inner self. When you do that it is amazing how often the outer life takes on a different hue.

It is worth remembering the wise simplicity of one approach to what constitutes prayer and meditation. Whatever techniques are employed, in prayer there is a questing, an asking; in meditation at its core there is waiting and listening for the answer or answers.

Children (of all ages) need time in which they are not expected to perform, produce, behave or learn – in play they will hear what's inside themselves

This is about expectations, and giving ourselves the gift of time to be free of them. From our earliest moments we are in training, not just to survive but also, as it appears, to get the love we crave. At first it appears that we are in charge. We let the world know in a loud voice that we need feeding and the breast, bottle, or spoonful arrives sooner or later. We poop in our well-padded pants whenever and wherever we want to, and it's accepted as the norm. We fall asleep anywhere, anytime, and it's just fine.

Learning comes automatically, actually it's more like absorption, and we adjust to what is acceptable in our immediate environment and in the community in which we live. In other words we learn what is expected of us to get what we need to survive. Whether or not those expectations are in line with what we *want* is another matter, the seeds are sown.

The conditioning continues as we encounter more of the outside world and, typically, the school environment amplifies the need to perform, produce, behave and learn continually. Where is the play? The permission and the time for it get less and less.

Let's be clear – this is not about trying to resolve the old 'nature versus nurture' argument, they're not mutually exclusive anyway. The learned survival kit is present in all of us. This is not a judgement of its contents, it is simply an acknowledgement of its existence and of the power of the expectations within it to become internalised and limit our capacity to play in later life. Often even what appears to be play has a goal, a purpose, built in. Games and sports for all ages incorporate building something, creating something, self improvement, winning. All perfectly laudable, but all reinforcing the end product rather than the means.

This may come as a timely reminder to you to take time out to play. The value of doing, or not doing, for the sheer pleasure of the moment, with no end in view, and preferably with others or one other at least. The plural seems to be an integral part of this energy, but don't let the lack of it stop you from playing.

Take a few moments to think, to feel, what would be playful for you. What can you do, or be, which involves no goal or purpose in doing it or being it? Play is its own reward, and there may be a bonus in putting aside the residual expectations for a while, namely that doing so can allow you to become aware of some inner truths which have been waiting for the opportunity to surface. Don't go looking for them though, they will either come or they won't – just play!

Sometimes not getting what you want is the greatest gift

If this text has surfaced for you, it has probably been accompanied by a groan of despair, or at least a sigh of resignation. Let's have a look at how the apparent negative can indeed be a gift.

Not getting what we want is an area of denial with which we are all familiar. From our earliest days the in–built desire for gratification surfaces. It has never been more evident than it is in today's consumer led society. Surrounded by an embarrassment of riches, children's cries of 'I want', 'I want', 'I want …', reverberate around supermarkets and shopping centres, and adults are following the same drives except the identical cries have become internalised and largely unspoken.

At another level it could be said that those early appeals are also asking for boundaries to be set, for however broadly or narrowly they are drawn we all need some clear negative responses along the way to define the limits of personal territory. If all the early 'I wants' are gratified the result is usually an unhappy, unbounded child, and eventually a perpetually dissatisfied, frustrated adult who is unable to deal with or accept limitations on his/her desires or behaviour.

So, the first advantage of not always getting what you want is a basis for psychological good health. There are many other factors of course, but we all need boundaries, and with them comes at least the possibility of acceptance of existing circumstances, and with acceptance, peace. Paradoxically, barriers and obstacles can fall away, or be transformed, the easier, once their existence has been accepted and embraced as part of your reality.

Another possibility is that life is prompting you to change direction. There may be something, or someone, you have been pursuing fruitlessly for some time, and this text is suggesting that you put your energies into different goals. Not getting what you want can feel like banging your head against a solid wall and there may be an opening in the wall if you take a few steps sideways.

On an energetic level the presence of strong desire can actually repel the object of that desire. How? Consider for a moment. If you want something, what are you affirming? That you haven't got it now – and guess what, the universe gets in line with that clear statement in the moment and keeps the desired result at a distance.

It's time to let go a major desire in your life, and if you really let go, without looking back, what then has a chance to come into that cleared space may be even better than your original desire – but don't go looking for that either, you'll simply fill up that space again.

You may have had quite enough of not getting what you want, so much so that you are ready to give up the struggle to get it. Enough already! If this is the case, the gifts that arise in response to genuine surrender can be awesome, from the simple everyday to the mystical.

The text is laying out for you one of the classic 'through the negative to the positive' processes which is applicable to your life right now. Open yourself to the greatest gift.

Angels can fly because they take themselves lightly

There is a wonderful scene in the evergreen film 'Mary Poppins' in which the act of laughing takes the characters up towards the ceiling. You are probably in need of something similar, and particularly if you can laugh at yourself. Tell your serious self to take some time off.

Alright, you don't necessarily have to laugh out loud, although that would be a delightful bonus, but look for the humour in situations rather than deep meaning and significance. You know you're good at the serious stuff of life, well you've been applying yourself in that way for a tad too long, it's time to get your feet off the ground, or even elevate them from the mud of that survival rut which may have you held fast.

There are millions, if not billions of words written about enlightenment. Well here are a few more. How about taking the word literally. It could be used as a comparative term. If you find the means to feel lighter about life, yourself, or some situation, then compared to your former state you are literally enlightened are you not.

There is no doubt that life can feel burdensome at times, in the western world probably most of the time – the acquisition of money and possessions means the devotion of ever increasing time and energy to their pursuit, maintenance, and improvement. The resultant responsibilities can be perceived as a burden to be carried, baggage which can become unbearably heavy.

The same can be said of any drive, however legitimate. The religious and philosophical need to know can get bogged down in intellectual weight. The drive to self knowledge, self discovery, awareness can lead to the attempt to see deep meaning and significance in every little action and reaction. The same applies in relationship, family, work. Any of this sound familiar?

It's time to stand back and look at yourself with a readiness to see the lighter side, you may need someone close to you who can operate the necessary probe, a kind of mental and emotional tickler!

Who can doubt that angels are enlightened beings? How appropriate it is that they are so often depicted with glorious wings. It matters not if you believe in them as a reality or a figment of the imagination, for the moment your best interests are served by the symbology of their existence.

Burdens we all have, perhaps the angels have as well. The choice we have is to carry the weight of them heavily or lightly. There's the inherent duality of life giving us a choice again. Imagine your wings coming out in sympathy with a smile; even emerging in all their glory when you laugh.

Choose the incredible lightness of being which you are capable of, direct some of it at yourself, and lift off, even if it's only a few inches!

Gratitude opens the heart

Here is an apt reminder of the power of gratitude, which flies in the face of so much about the society in which we live. The path of least resistance seems to be to concentrate on the negatives, the apparent problems, and the needs of victimhood which requires something or someone to blame.

This is a time for you to turn away from that slippery slope, from that programming which can wield such power in the psyche, from the ever present head trip which keeps it in place. Such concentration of attention, continually reinforced by all forms of media and our obsessional attachment to the negatives tend to be heart closers, and it is time for you to cry 'enough'.

There is always something for which giving thanks is appropriate. It may be that your gratitude is objective and can be directed specifically toward someone or something, singular or plural. Equally it could be subjective and generalised, like simply being grateful to be alive. Even if only in odd moments, there is so much benefit to be had in turning away from the shadows that have become so comfortable toward the light that is comforting instead.

Opening the book here is a guarantee that you can find much to prompt a move to the heart from the head and feel the gratitude just waiting to be realised.

One apt definition is simply that gratitude is prayer, and the following is intended as an aid to the energy present in you right now. If all of the following applies then you are indeed fortunate. Some of it will without doubt. Whatever you find in these words appropriate to you, rejoice in what they reflect about you and let the gratitude flow in. At the very least you will be pleasantly surprised at what is engendered within you.

A PRAYER OF THANKSGIVING

I have food in my belly, when so many are starving.
I have space of my own, when so many are homeless.
I breathe freely, when so many fight for breath.
I can walk as a youth, when so many are immobile.
I can see, when so many are blind.
I can hear an infinitude of sound, when so many are deaf.
I can speak my thoughts, when so many are denied that freedom.
My heart is full of life, when so many are shackled to
early death.
No matter the storms of life, mental and emotional balance
always return.
No matter my ego demands and denials, I am aware of the gift
and presence of love in my life.
No matter my social or financial status, I am blessed.
I am deeply grateful, and gratitude is my daily prayer.

How good can I stand it today?

The only possible restriction on good things coming your way right now is your ability to receive them. This is one of those times in the cycles of living when the statement 'If it's not one thing it's another!', often expressed in exasperated reaction to apparent negatives, can be felt and expressed with a welcoming smile to the positives being presented.

The awareness required here is to do with our traditional attachment to the negative as being predominant in our lives. All kinds of statements and decisions about ourselves often form unnecessarily tight boundaries on our ability to enjoy the bounty of life when it comes our way, apparently without effort on our part.

There's a whole heap of stuff in there, some of which you may resonate with at this time. 'I don't deserve it.' 'I can't have what I want.' 'No, I couldn't possibly.' 'I'm not good enough.' 'I don't matter.' 'I'm not ready.' 'I don't want to know.' 'I can't do this.' 'I have to do everything myself'.

There are many more of similar ilk which are deeply embedded in our psychological blueprint and they all contribute to a structure of low self esteem and/or denial, which, in turn, can make us cling to the life contracting and habitually refuse the life expanding opportunities when they come along. This is a time to be aware of any such tendencies in yourself, bring them up to consciousness, have a chat with them and tell them their predominance is on hold for the moment!

An analogy coming up. It is as if, for a time at least, the clouds at different levels of your life – physical, emotional, mental – have moved aside from the sun, and you have a choice. You can either 1) cover up from top to toe, put on a wide brimmed hat and top strength sun tan lotion, and head for the nearest shade, or 2) strip off, leave the protection aside, and frolic in the sun knowing, for once, there is no chance of you getting burned. It's a challenge. You're used to the shade, can you stand it in the light?

Another mindset which need not hold sway over you, for the moment at least, is the one that demands that you have to work hard for anything you want or value. 'No pain, no gain' just about sums it up. Right now life is trying to bring you gifts for which no expenditure of effort is required. If that's hard to accept, believe that what is flowing your way constitutes reward for past efforts – for these gifts you've already done what is necessary.

So, how good is good? What are we talking about here? Observe the various levels of your life. It could be there are opportunities for positive changes in physical circumstances. You may simply feel good about yourself and life at the moment and it's enough to enjoy that feeling. You may have a period of exceptional mental clarity about a situation where formerly there has been confusion.

Spiritually you may feel inspired, and be getting clues from your intuition that you are on the right track, or any combination of the above. Suffice it to say, you are blessed. Count the ways.

Divine discontent beckons through the mists of personal agenda

This may be the harbinger of a profound change in the way you hold life, and your part in it. The deepest shift in consciousness is that which accompanies the transcendence of the self – that's the self with a small 's'. It could be called the ego, a set of survival patterns, that part of us which wants to define and defend its individuality. (Isn't it interesting that the word individuality includes 'duality' so even within the identity which we prize there is the divided self).

That doesn't mean you defeat it, or it disappears for ever. No, the self still appears to be present, the transcendent state simply means that you no longer identify with it, and from your new viewpoint you see that its apparent reality is, and always has been, an illusion. A time to be in the world but not of it. Being who and what you are is not a function of doing; doing is a function of being.

Let's backtrack. If you resonate with the first part of this little gem then which part of you is capable of registering unhappiness? Isn't it the part which wants some part of your life, or life in general, to be different from the way it is? And would that not be yet another good description of the self which, of itself, is not capable of the acceptance and surrender to what *is* which is necessary for transcendence?

The glimpses of the Oneness of all things, of the Self, which may be beckoning you right now, or very soon, are revealing the immutable 'Isness', the unchangeable, uncontrollable content and perfection of the moment. From that place the degree of our motivations which are indeed self-centred become obvious simultaneously with the recognition of what is real and what is illusion. The value of discontent can be to bring our attention to the difference between the two.

This is not intended as a judgement of being self-centred. It is legitimate in the order of things. It is not right or wrong to be self-centred. It is necessary to our experience of life at certain levels. However there will always come a time when a greater experience calls us and this time is present or imminent in you.

It is not something you can make happen, or force in any way. It may come in the form of a mystical experience, a burst of irresistible inspiration, or a steady state which underpins your life – and that steady state could be a pain right now. However it makes its presence felt it is always a wake up call; you will know that the obsessions of the persona are but an illusion.

Let go the psychopomp teacher!

This is a good time to shut up! If there are genuine questions coming your way, or if there is an invitation to speak your truth, then by all means share what you know. Otherwise, keep it to yourself. This is not the time to spill the beans as you know them. If you do, you are more likely to prompt alienation than any other response.

There has been an explosion of interest in the exploration of self in recent years. The need to know more about who we are, what drives us, what makes us behave the way we do, has prompted many to delve beneath the surface of purely physiological or material answers. Often we are bound to find that the latter come up short, not just intellectually either.

There is a growing awareness that what dictates the real quality of life, once basic survival needs are taken care of, comes welling up from within. How do we really feel? Do we have much idea of who we really are and what we're doing here? What is our experience of ourselves beyond the rationalisation and the never ending judgements?

As an increasing minority has dipped toes in these waters, or dived in if that is your way, personal knowledge of the human condition has grown. You may have attended seminars, groups, courses, worked with various approaches and therapies, become attached to a guru or teacher.

Whatever form it takes you know a lot more about yourself than when you started. A natural result of this process is that you want to share what you have learned. That's fine and dandy, but you have to develop discrimination as to where and when you do that. Uninvited evangelism is a pain.

It may be everything you have learned and experienced is purely for your own growth and development. and not necessarily for dissemination. The only person you are responsible for changing is yourself and, who knows, by so doing you may be serving others as best you may without ever expressing the urge to teach.

Be assured, if it is in your destiny, you will get your chance to speak, to communicate what you know. The current lesson is to wait for that chance, to wait for the question, to wait for the invitation to make your contribution, and if they do not come – this is a time to keep quiet.

If you are making real progress in your psychological process, if you are becoming more whole, expanding into more of what it really means to be a human being, then your presence alone will make people wonder about you and want to ask questions. If they sense peace in you when they have none, or very little, in themselves, they will ask questions sooner or later, and right now you have to wait for them.

Remember your essential innocence

A cloak of regret, remorse even, has descended on you. You may have thought something, felt something, done something, which has prompted you to take on a burden of guilt. Let's expand the limits of the apparently separate, suffering ego. In the language of duality, guilt and innocence exist as opposites, yet even at this level innocence is so much more than simply a state of being not guilty. An acceptance of true personal responsibility can, ironically, move us toward the reality of our greater Innocence.

The concept of personal responsibility is not a question of attaching blame or fault as in the language of victimhood. No, it is beyond victimhood into a state of acceptance of consequences. It is accepting that the energy system which constitutes a human being will always draw to itself the manifestation of that which will balance perfectly the output, conscious or unconscious, of that system.

Far from being a negative concept therefore, personal responsibility recognises that whatever the consequences they are always in some way a loving reflection of what the persona needs to maintain or return to a state of balance. You can heap self blame on your shoulders if you like, but if you can accept personal responsibility you are far beyond the issues of blame and fault, you are ready to accept the consequences of natural law. That which is yours will always return to you; that which you take will always be taken from you.

Now take another step toward the truth of this text, which is about true and ultimate Innocence. However you are at the level of duality, of personality, of ego, whatever you've done or think you've done, whatever degree of personal responsibility you've accepted, you're always playing a role, acting a part. You are not the doer. The ego believes it is the doer and suffers the agonies of guilt attaching to that belief. You are being presented with an antidote to your guilt, a reminder that everything is ultimately divinely created, directed and acted, no exceptions.

'All the world's a stage...' and all that. At one level that is literally true. We are players, actors, who are so seduced by the role we are playing, called personality, that we believe we are in control of the script, the stage directions, the props, even the other players. It's a kind of addiction that we all suffer from, until life shows us we're not in control of anything, then we stand a chance of enjoying the role we're playing. There is an apt saying – 'If life gives you lemons, make lemonade!' All life is divinely Innocent, and that includes you.

'You've never done anything. You never have and you never will. If ever you think you have, remember, I am the playwright, the play, and the players, and your part has been written for all eternity.'

Choose tenderly a place for thine academy

There is a commitment in you to a deeper purpose than your everyday survival. Just as a pregnancy is a time of waiting to bring forth a new being in physical form, you are 'pregnant' with a project, an idea, a creation of your own, waiting the time and place to bring it to fruition. Don't give up on it, the necessary quality of energy required has not appeared as yet. Whatever the project, it deserves to be brought forth, it has value for you and for others, and the appearance of that quality is imminent.

It may be the commitment to 'know thyself' on the road to personal liberation, in which case it is time for you to choose your route carefully, don't rush it, listening to the heart takes more patience than listening to your head. Sometimes we have to wait for the head to exercise its prerogative over the process of evaluation, weighing up the pros and cons, doing its bit to solve the problem – often when there is no problem save that which it has created to justify its existence.

Then when the shot and shell has died down, the heart can make itself felt in its own gentle, loving way and assert what was always going to be anyway. If you need another to reflect your state of being or your progress, a mentor, a teacher, a therapist, a guru, take the time to feel who is right for you. Choose tenderly.

You may have felt for some time that a time of study is calling you, perhaps with some uncertainty about how to bring this about. Remember the energy with you now is related to deeper purpose. What you study, where and when, is not necessarily concerned with worldly pursuits. The results are most likely to be of benefit to your connection with who you really are rather than simply a means to create a bigger income. The rewards will be recognised more by the inner self than the demands of the outer life. Choose tenderly.

You may be approaching a time of withdrawal, of retreat, feeling the need to go within, a time of meditation, in which case this is a reminder to prepare for that. Put your affairs in order as much as you can so they are not attachments dragging you back from your primary goal. At the same time be aware that there are hooks and ropes in all that demands to be put in order, and particularly now when much may be crowding in on you, forcing you to think of a haven of retreat from it all. Choose a time and space to withdraw and during that time let all that your mind insists on bringing to your attention bang away at the door of your consciousness unheeded. Choose tenderly.

Let the choice emerge whether or not you need to move to another location for this time with yourself, or can it be best achieved right where you are. Choose tenderly.

The only person you are responsible for changing is yourself

At first sight this maxim smacks of a kind of selfish exclusivity with the negative connotations so often attached to that descriptive adjective 'selfish'. In fact, it could be argued that anything we ever do has a 'pay off' at some level, but that's another story. No, if you are ready for this, and you must be otherwise you wouldn't have opened the book here, realising this energy within yourself can make a profound difference to the quality of life.

You may have been going through a time of trying to make your life function better by attempting to control or change someone else. It might be habitual in your scheme of things to do that. Could you be labelled a control freak? Has it been a case of 'My way or the highway'? Firstly, that response is in us all to some extent, and until we learn otherwise we try and control outer circumstances, including other people, as a way of making life feel safer for us – it's a knee jerk survival fear reaction. Secondly, it doesn't work does it, and that may be coming home to you.

There is a resonance here with the first of the twelve steps of the Alcoholics Anonymous recovery programme, which is now seen to have application to many other addictive behaviours. There is an acknowledgement of powerlessness over others which, paradoxically, leads to the birth of self–empowerment and looking within to one's own reality rather than trying to adjust and change the lives of others.

It's not a new concept, but look at the word responsibility in terms of the ability to respond. As awareness increases it is possible to see the difference between reacting and responding. The former tends to be compulsive, set in the concrete of old behaviour patterns. The latter appears to have within it more choice, springing from the present day awareness.

So often we react to others, even if we have adjusted our outer action, the inner reaction still makes its presence felt. However, we always have the ability to respond, responsibility, to ourselves and thereby change by conscious choice the only person on this planet that we can change.

If you really get this message, there is a tremendous release, a letting go of potential conflict within and without. People do what they do, say what they say, behave in accordance with their perceived reality which is always going to be different from yours.

It's time to let go believing you can do anything about that. The irony is, the way this amazing game of life is set up, as you accept that the only person you are responsible for changing is yourself, and you attend to your own inner reality, just watch how the mirror of your outer life, and the people in it seem to change without any direct intervention on your part.

Live your life
and watch what comes to you –
your deepest desires are known

This is about opening up your powers of observation. There is a great deal of literature and meditative experience about being the witness, watching the richness of the inner life. This is about watching the abundance of the outer life, or what is apparently outer.

At one level it is all inner experience. However, for present purposes we will make the separation and say that observing the content of the outer life is what you need to do right now. It would be reasonable to say 'I'm always doing that anyway!' Right now that is open to question.

What we tend to do is identify with the outer contents of our lives. In other words we get so caught up with them, so attached to them, they become the whole focus and measure of who we are. For some, identifying with conditions at home for example means that if home is dirty and disordered, they will feel dirty and disordered; if home is clean and tidy, they will feel personally clean and tidy.

That's what is meant by identifying with the outer. It could be relationship, family, work, or any number of things which push and pull our sense of ourselves in many different directions. In that state it is difficult, if not impossible, to observe, to watch, to witness. It would be like asking the eye to look at itself. There is a need to take a step back and become aware of who and what is coming your way. You don't have to set out to change anything, or react in a different way, in fact efforts to do so would probably get in the way. Be aware of so called coincidence in your life, it may be significant.

Duality of mind, and the need to judge will make what comes to you good or bad, positive or negative, joyful or sad, and so on. Whilst all that categorising is going on, which it will, see if you can observe it all at the same time. Witness your objective life dispassionately in the certain knowledge that, in some way, everything is attempting to contribute to the fulfilment of your deepest desires. You may not even know what your deepest desires are, then watching what comes to you may give you some clues. They may not be even obvious and conscious desires, in which case they will be subtle and sub–conscious ones.

The contribution may not be obvious in the short term, it will become so in the long term. The answer is to trust life, even if it appears to be dealing you some pretty awful cards. An Intelligence greater than yours is doing its best to give you what you want, and that includes sometimes bringing you experiences which, when fully embraced, are necessary to clear the way to your deepest desires. 'Stay the course. Somebody may be reminding you that they have you in mind.'

We live in a world created and maintained by desire in all its forms, from the simplest to the most sublime, and rest assured, yours are in there registered energetically since the beginning of time.

Do what you love and love what you do

This kind of terminology makes us think of what we do for a living. The profession or occupation by which we earn the money to survive, or even prosper, on a day to day basis is what is behind the enquiry 'What do you do?'

Some kind of shift is required in your approach to what you do to generate income. It may be that there is much to keep you in an apparent straitjacket of necessity which compels work that is less than satisfying. It may be that you feel you have to occupy your day with work you don't love so that you are enabled to do what you *do* love outside the working environment.

You may have studied, trained, qualified in your profession, and have discovered that being good at what you do doesn't guarantee that you love doing it. It is possible to have such ingrained denial of yourself or of life itself that even when there is sufficient time and money to do what you love, you still find reasons not to do it.

It is time to identify what you love doing. It may be currently a hobby, something you do in your 'spare' time. It may be an activity you have noticed others doing and felt 'I would love to do that'.

What is it, when in prospect, makes you feel excited, looking forward to doing it. Imagine feeling like that about the working day. It can be that way. You are ready to make the shift and either make a change straight away, or start the process of moving toward doing what you love. There is a breakthrough to be made.

It may be an internal one initially which leads to determination, a commitment to do what you love doing more and more, however that looks. The beauty of it is, as enjoyment manifests in what you're doing, the more likely it will be for money to come in. Money is just a symbol of the movement of energy so any negative attitudes or feelings in your space will act as blocks to the flow. Whereas, loving what you do facilitates the flow of energy so the money will fly to you! For that, it might be worth taking a few risks.

Equally, if there really is no way of changing what you do, for the moment at least, then bring some love to it every day. There may be much in your current work to provoke negative reactions. Whatever the judgements, attitudes, feelings are, they are inside you, the content of the work itself is never the cause, you can choose to do what is required of you from a different perspective. Don't get sucked into the form – the form is ultimately neutral – it is in your power to bring love or hate to the task.

Life is a function of duality, so wherever you see much to be *against* there will be always be an equal amount to be *for*. Bring your potential for love and joy to your current situation and you will be able to find and focus on positive aspects of what you are doing. That is the stuff of transformation, which always comes from within not without.

Loving what you do creates a different experience of whatever you have to do, and remember not to beat yourself up when you catch yourself dwelling on the negatives again, there's a process going on here, give yourself time, and witness the results.

'He who binds to himself a joy, Does the winged life destroy; But he who kisses the joy as it flies, Lives in eternity's sun rise'

This is a profound little piece by the poet and mystic William Blake. In a nutshell it's about the drawbacks of attachment and the advantages of non-attachment.

When the flow of life brings to us an experience, a sensation, a feeling which is pleasurable, joyful, brings us moments of happiness, the tendency is to try and repeat exactly the circumstances which appeared to bring it about. In other words we become attached to a time and place with things, activities and people – a whole scenario if you like – which can never again be duplicated. Even if it could be, the energy of the moment has gone forever.

A young man leaps from an aircraft, having gathered his courage for his first attempt at skydiving. In the few seconds before his parachute opens his experience moves beyond time and space, he is in 'the zone' if you like, he knows nothing and everything in that everlasting moment. He lands safely and thereafter becomes a passionate devotee of skydiving, hoping to repeat that enlightening experience – and he never does, at least not through repetition of leaping out of aircraft.

Whether the situation is life-changing, or a moment in the everyday, we live in a time/space system in which the essence of life is movement, flow. Scientists have long since recognised that everything which occupies space in the universe has qualities, characteristics, boundaries which define its apparently separate, unique existence. What is not generally recognised, except perhaps by mystics and astrologers, is that the same applies to each moment in time, each moment is unique and unrepeatable with qualities all its own.

Whatever the experience you have just had, or, indeed, may still be having, feel it, enjoy it, and let it go. It could be as simple as the response to seeing a butterfly on a rose, or as profound as having a glimpse of the oneness of all life, the mystic experience beyond words – it matters not – kiss the joy as it flies.

If you do that you will be making way for all the other unique moments coming your way, and the unknown and unknowable joys they contain to come to you. On the other hand, if you try and hang on to what any part of the flow brings you then you create a log jam of thoughts, feelings, expectations which prevent the fullness of the next moment, the next joy from reaching you.

If there is a joy, a beauty, a profundity in your life at the moment, don't try and work it out, analyse it to death, repeat it by conscious effort or control it. Let it be exactly the way it is, embrace it and let it go, with love and gratitude.

Authentic teachers of my truth must have enough humility to lean completely on my strength and stay within their closet until I open the door

The use of the first person in this quotation indicates that this is channelled material from a source greater than the small 'I' of the personality. Whether or not you believe in that source or, indeed, that it could communicate in this way is largely irrelevant because opening the book here can still be a pointer to what is going on in your energy field.

This is a time in human history when a huge leap in consciousness is occurring. Transition, transformation, call it what you will, is not about changing or overthrowing existing political, economic, or social systems for actual or apparent material gain of one sort or another. Technological revolution, or any other kind of revolution changes the outer expression of life, not necessarily the inner experience of it. There are more people than ever on this planet who are still struggling simply to survive. No, we are talking evolution, not revolution.

A vital part of what is taking place now is the revelation of esoteric knowledge at many levels. The real truths of the human condition which transcend rational, left brain logic and understanding, which go way beyond mere intellectual grasp and philosophical discussion, have always been known to a few, a tiny minority of enlightened individuals throughout the ages. Genuine masters, gurus, shamans, keepers of secret mystic traditions at the heart of all major religions, to name some of the few. Now the doors are opening. What has been hidden can not be hidden any longer. Holistic knowing, rather than just understanding, is available to those who seek it and who are not afraid to open up their right brain receptivity to intuition and inspiration, and their heart's capacity to feel and therefore to love, without effort to do so.

You may well be one of those who have knocked on the door and it has opened, at least part of the way. At the centre of what you have discovered exists, by its very nature, a deep desire to share what you know, to teach others so they may benefit from your knowledge.

The message for you is clear – not yet. If it is in your destiny to do so, then the opportunities will come, be it with one other person at a time or 'when two or more are gathered together'. You can't force it. It has a timing all its own which is beyond your control. A greater Intelligence than your own will know when to let you loose on the world!

In the meantime use what you have gained for your own refinement, and for your own increasing alignment with love rather than fear.

If it feels nice, don't think twice!

A large proportion of the statements and decisions about life and ourselves which we hold most dear, our attitudes, our belief systems, our shoulds and oughts, our mental construct if you like, are restrictive. Generation after generation has passed on versions of 'Do this, don't do that; you can feel this, but it's not alright to feel that, you can think this, but not that.'

The trouble is that, whatever the variations, the mindset thus formed becomes a powerful, if not dominant, part of our persona. It sets rules and regulations which don't allow much room for play. In the interests of survival and control, the flow of life is channelled, restricted, curtailed according to the prosecutor, judge and jury permanently residing in the supreme court of the head.

All too often the life sentence calls for work, duty, responsibility, achievement, success, constancy, putting others before oneself, and so on. Nothing wrong with any of that, until and unless there is no room for anything else including your humble self. It's time for a bit of balance. Time for the cell door to open, for a while at least. You've been a model prisoner for long enough. There needs to be a mass breakout – of your senses.

With this energy around, be aware of opportunities which may come your way to simply feel nice. The tentacles of the conditioned mindset often obscure what pleasures life is attempting to give you at this time. The Latin phrase *carpe diem* comes to mind – seize the day.

Now you are being put on notice that the time is ripe for you to let your hair down and indulge yourself. Let your senses and desires take over. For the moment it will be just fine for you to be sensual.

That means looking at someone or something for the sheer pleasure of looking – no goal in mind. Smelling the roses, or lilies, or a favourite food cooking, whatever, for the heaven in the scent. Enjoying the tastes of indulgent mouthfuls of anything that takes your fancy. Listening to sounds which reach you, which move you. Being tactile with whoever or whatever feels good against your skin. Get into your body and your feelings – they're always in the moment. Right now there doesn't have to be a result, an end product. There's nothing to achieve.

Your internal judge and jury may go crazy – fine, let them, this is not their time. They will make their presence felt with a wealth of familiar thoughts about such self indulgence on your part. Thank them for their contribution, then close the doors to the courtroom. They will still be ranting on when you re–open for business. There's a great big world outside their domain and it's time for you to enjoy more of it, so if it feels nice, go for it!

Isn't our normal routine the unexpected?

This is a time in your life to expect the unexpected. It may come at you from any direction, and just when you think you are prepared for it you are still taken by surprise, or don't even notice it for what it is.

Much depends on your mindset right now. One way or another your applecart is about to be upset and you can see it as a confounded nuisance, an obstacle to your ordered life, and try and put the apples back exactly the way they were before. Alternatively, you can regard it as an opportunity, a wake up call perhaps, to prompt an adjustment in an area of your life which may have become stagnant. To continue the metaphor, do you still want to be trading in apples anyway?!

It may well be that much of your life has become a matter of habit. Often when we think we are making choices, they are not free choices at all, but they are simply guiding us along well defined and familiar grooves. It has been said that a rut differs from a grave only in depth. Sometimes life serves us with the unexpected as an opportunity, firstly, to recognise that some part of our lives has become habitual, addictive even; and secondly, as a clue to the new direction.

The arrival of the unexpected doesn't have to be huge. It may be the equivalent of a volcanic eruption, but it may just as easily be a chance meeting, or a telephone call out of the blue, or a gentle realisation of something which has been staring you in the face for some time. Ultimately it is impossible to define because of its very nature. If we could define it and prepare for it, then it wouldn't be the unexpected would it!

All you can do, with the help of this text, is be prepared for your inner reactions. They could be any combination of emotions, surprise, elation, pleasure, excitement, apprehension, fear. Whatever it is for you, recognition is now more likely, so there is a better chance of welcome and integration.

Be aware that everything, every scenario, large or small, represents life attempting to contribute to your liberation in some way. The surprises, the unexpected, the bolt from the blue coming your way will be another invitation from the Beloved to join in the divine game of life. Every apparent negative has the positive within it, every positive has its negative counterpart. We function in duality, so the unexpected will be judged to be one or the other. However briefly, you can move into the unity beyond duality. The tree that bends with the wind does not judge the wind, or the direction from which it comes, it simply bends and includes the new experience. This is a time for you to be as that tree.

Let your presence be a blessing

You have reached a stage where the role you are called upon to play may not be the lead or even an apparently minor part, but appearances are deceptive. At last the awareness has dawned of the value of simply being who and what you are.

Continual exposure to the pain and dysfunction of others may have brought it home to you that the space you occupy is not nearly so troubled, not nearly so diseased as the vast majority of humankind seems to be. Indeed you are coming to know, perhaps only in intermittent periods of time as yet, what it means to be truly peaceful – a state you have sought all your life.

You have known the treadmills of striving to attain, probably material security initially, and when that didn't do it for you, you may have swapped treadmills for the one which is equally goal oriented but marked psychological and/or spiritual. Worthy though they both are, the seeker remains, and you are ready to step off both means of prolonging the agony.

This may well be where you are now. You tried achieving outwardly, you may even have reaped the rewards of your efforts, but that proved an empty promise. Then you delved deeply into achieving inwardly, and though that apparent journey gave you increased self-knowledge, it still left an apparent void. Lo and behold, the void is where it is, where it has always been, waiting for you to drop in!

Goals and achieving, growing, progressing, moving on, are all products of the conditioned mind. Nothing wrong with that; it has to be that way, with all its illusions, so that the dualistic drama of life can continue. However, where you are now is a condition of the heart not the head. It performs its life giving service for the most part unnoticed, unsung, maintaining very existence without goals, without paths to follow, without trying to improve itself, and all the while carrying the weight of all the thinking, emoting, and doing imposed upon it, often to its eventual detriment when function becomes dysfunction.

Indeed, research has revealed that deep inside the tissues of the heart there are neurons, which are associated with long term memory in the brain. So science is discovering what mystics have always known, that the heart has a 'mind', or rather a consciousness of its own.

What you have 'achieved' is beyond price. There is a knowing burgeoning within you that you are all you need to be, and that brings with it an acceptance, a peace, a serenity even, which pervades your energy, which gives you a presence. Doing is not necessary – it will happen, life will go on at every level and you will still participate in that doing, but now you know that no effort is necessary for you to make a valuable contribution, for this is a contribution at the energetic level.

The energy you take with you does not depend on what you do, but what you are; it is effortless, serene, and of the heart. You don't have to set out to teach, or even heal, as an outward expression, but that expression of your energy may well take place as others are drawn to you as the thirsty are drawn to a well. And in the middle of that ease you have sought, that peace that passeth all understanding, you can be content that indeed, your presence alone is a blessing. Rest easy in that sublime service.

Take risks, the net only appears when you're in mid-air

So much of the society we have created seems driven to make life safe and comfortable, and that would appear to be a legitimate aim. However, if life is to be fulfilling, if satisfaction rather than gratification is what we crave, then attempting to be safe and comfortable all the time will tend to produce nothing more than habitual survival behaviour and attitudes. It is said that a rut differs from a grave only in depth, and yet how often do we accept the confines of our particular rut in the interests of being safe and comfortable. Is it satisfying, fulfilling? Perhaps not.

Consider the humble rabbit. Predators abound for its succulent flesh, yet even to survive it has to emerge from its burrow in order to eat. It has to go beyond the limits of maximum safety in order to continue being a rabbit! A situation which abounds throughout the animal kingdom.

Are we so very different from Mr. Rabbit? Humankind is expansionist by nature, and however much we resist it, life is always presenting the opportunities for new experiences, new faces, new places. Growth and development are the current obsessions of the western world, in fact they are increasingly taking over the whole world. They appear constantly in universal terms, and also in the personal.

Opening the book here indicates that the time is ripe for you to expand your existing boundaries in some way. However that presents itself to you it is bound to feel risky. Risk is a very personal thing – what feels normal and everyday to one will appear to be a tremendous risk to another. For the writer, speaking in public is a pleasure and a joy and doesn't feel in the least bit risky, yet the reverse is true for many others. For some, and you may be one of them, simply asking for what you want sometimes can feel like an enormous risk. There is no absolute measure.

Be aware of any potential for movement from the familiar to the unfamiliar. It is a time for your patterns to be challenged, for some flexibility to be introduced to a life situation which has become too rigid. It doesn't have to be earth shaking or deeply philosophical. It is often in the everyday and can be as simple as saying how you really feel about something or someone. Do what you have always done, and you will get what you have always got.

There are times when you are called upon simply to endure. This is <u>not</u> one of those times. There will be opportunities for you to say something or do something which will create the potential for change, and you will recognise the window of opportunity because there will be fear of the consequences – otherwise it wouldn't feel risky! It may be taking the first steps toward a career move, a new relationship, or ending one, a new home, a creative project, a change in appearance. Great or small, the essence for you right now is contained within the thought 'Go on, take a risk.'

By moving into the unknown voluntarily, consciously you will be pushing out the boundaries of who you are. That is personal growth. In energy terms you will be literally larger than you were, and the universe has to respond to that. To encompass that expansion the structure of support has to adjust to the new you, in other words the net appears!

Let your heart break, for therein lies the love that transforms, awaiting release

When we talk of a broken heart we are attempting to articulate extreme emotional pain. Putting that into words is always going to be inadequate to express the intensity of feeling which is present. You may be experiencing the affects of personal loss, separation, or betrayal, perhaps all three, or whatever the catalyst is for your deepest, most hurtful feelings to be moved into a dominant place in your consciousness.

As always, it appears that there is a choice at such moments. How many times have you heard, or, indeed, said to yourself 'Life must go on', and that normally means that you 'stuff' or repress the feelings and immerse yourself in the everyday minutiae of physical survival. Trying to hold everything together at a time like this is one of the toughest challenges we have to face.

The suggestion here is that there is another way, another choice. Instead of holding on to what the rational mind judges to be sanity, which is often closer to insanity at times like these; instead of repressing, or avoiding the feelings; let them speak their truth. What does that mean? Internally, it means you stop resisting their existence and allow yourself to feel the strength of their presence. The latter can mean a physical sensation somewhere in the body – not just tension, that's the symptom of holding on – go behind the tension and see if you can sense what is being held in place.

For example, grief can feel like a heavy weight dragging on a body part, say, like a lead cloak around the heart, a weight in the chest restricting your breathing. You may feel sick, not want to eat at all. There may be a need to shake or shiver which you never realised was there. Deep emotions surfacing will be present in the body somewhere, see if you can locate them, not for the purpose of eradicating them, but simply to acknowledge their presence and to feel them.

Externally, you may need to find a safe time and space to express your heartbreak. An anecdote to illustrate this. A woman, grief stricken at recent personal loss, cried for weeks with no feeling of relief or an end to the mourning. Eventually, a therapist asked 'What do you really want to do, more than anything else, no holds barred?' The answer came 'I feel as if I want to go and howl at the moon!' The therapist said 'Fine, go do it!' So she did. She found a remote spot, well away from human eyes and ears, and on a moonlit night she allowed her feelings to speak their truth and howled at the moon. A profound peace entered the space previously filled by her deep unexpressed grief and she could move on with lighter step.

However you do it, here is a final thought in line with this aphorism. Why not let your heart break? What is the heart filled with, just waiting to be released? Love – and yet we have such resistance to it breaking out. Let it happen, and be liberated.

Divine love is about receiving, not giving. You just hold out your cup and let it be filled

So what's been getting in the way of you holding out your cup?! This is a timely reminder to you to let yourself receive. It is so easy for giving, putting yourself last, taking care of the needs and wants of others, serving in a way which depletes you, to become habitual. Often more obviously so if you are a woman, you have the double whammy of instinct plus conditioning.

Divine Onesong is always trying to sing to us. The flow of love is ever present, and it is like the sun shining, it gives life, light and warmth to everyone and everything, it does not discriminate. The problem is we put things in the way like tension, stress, denial, restrictive patterns, attachment to struggle and effort, conscious and unconscious thoughts and belief systems which project that we are undeserving or unworthy.

If the walls of Fort Self are in place and heavily defended we may keep out what appears to be threatening, but we also keep out the good stuff. Even compulsive giving can be a defence! Continuing the analogy, unless we open the gates occasionally to allow replenishment of essential stores, the fort collapses.

It is self evident that however much you enjoy giving, or feel compelled to do so, if it is always coming from personal energies and resources, without replenishment you will be drained, exhausted even, and thence unable to continue the giving. That is not only self-defeating, but in addition you can no longer give to those you seek to serve.

This text is indicating to you that maybe you have been giving too much, and it is time to redress the balance. All it takes is an internal shift in how you hold whatever comes your way. Stand on an imaginary bridge over the river of Life and see what comes downstream because right now there is nothing you can do to make the river flow any faster.

Much of what we take for granted could be held as gifts we can receive – the air we breathe, sunlight, moonlight, water in all its forms, the food we eat, the presence of those we hold dear – you get the idea. Now move into the personal. Are you an expert at diverting compliments? When someone says something nice about you do you immediately find a negative to nullify it, or rationalise it with a 'That's because......', or feel you have to return the compliment straight away? How about receiving it instead, saying 'Thank you', and letting it sit there in the cup you now hold up to be filled rather than continually holding it upside down.

A wise teacher and seminar leader has said 'Do you know when making love works best? When you are both receiving.' In similar fashion, the best healers are those who have learned to open themselves to receive when healing, then the flow of energy is unlimited, abundant. In both cases you know when you have been receiving because you feel energised afterward rather than drained.

One more thing. If we were all intent on giving all the time who is there to receive? By receiving you will be allowing someone else the pleasure of giving. In truth this whole game is set up to love you, support you, give to you, so you could hold out the biggest receptacle you could imagine, and it will still be filled – if you let it.

What has happened is all according to my wish. Offer me both merit earned and sin committed so that you may be liberated

This is a response from Divine Intelligence if ever there was one. You are likely to be either bathing in self congratulation or beating yourself up over imagined wrongdoings, usually the latter. Either way you are judging yourself about a significant event or change which is occurring or has just happened. An action or reaction in an area of your life that feels important is tending to dominate your waking hours right now.

The message is clear. Your judgements at this time are counter productive. It could be said that they are counter productive at any time. However your attachment to the apparent rights and wrongs of your handling of the current situation is tending to obstruct the flow of life more than usual. There's a sense of self-imprisonment. So whatever you think you've done, or not done, hand over those judgements to higher power, to the Source of all, to God, Great Spirit or however you define the Oneness behind all things.

Similarly, hand over the feelings which are likely to be attached to those judgements. There are no temporal paradigms applying to this aphorism. There may well be so called baggage from long ago which persists in making its presence felt again and again, and, lo and behold, here it is once more. Wherever you have placed personal responsibility for that past material, this page is telling you to hand over your part, real or imagined, to greater power. Surrender it, lock, stock, and barrel; let go, and the reward promised is huge – that you may be liberated.

What does that mean? It means that whenever the process of your life reminds you of what you see as 'merit earned' or 'sin committed' you will be at peace with it, there will no longer be a reaction to its appearance within or without – the memory will still be there, but the judgements and the feelings are minimal or non–existent.

What is emphasized here is the folly of believing we are in control. The survival mechanisms in the mind would have us believe that what happens is according to our wishes. They have a vested interest in maintaining the status quo, and that often includes judging ourselves according to belief systems and conditioning incurred long ago.

In any given moment the extent to which we identify with the mind is the extent to which we believe we are in control. No, the drive of this text stresses the reverse. Whatever has happened could not have been so without Divine assent. That's not approval or disapproval, our humanity always wants to add one or the other as a rider.

Divine Law always holds sway. The Beloved is present in all things. So surrender your judgements, it wasn't your doing anyway, and emerge from your prison cell into the light of day, the lightness of being which is liberation.

Authority only exists by consent

There are many forms of authority, and many forms of consent. As a subject for discussion the implications of these five words are endless. As applied universally, whole nations, societies, communities, any grouping or coming together of people, or animals come to that, will create a structure based on the essence of this text. Hierarchy emerges, and with hierarchy, authority. It would be reasonable to ask 'Where is the consent in a dictatorship or a totalitarian state?' It is still present, but based on fear and the need to survive.

However, these aphorisms are intended for personal guidance, not to provoke political discussion, so let's see how the above can apply to you. In a way we have all had experience of living in a dictatorship or a totalitarian state.

The whole process of growing up from new–born to apparent independence includes times of choiceless submission to authority. It may have been mother, father, siblings, teachers, and/or others who held that authority, and it is to be hoped that the apparent dictatorship was a benevolent one. Nevertheless, life is a function of duality so however the authority was applied, our perception of it would lend itself to times of willing consent, and times of unwilling consent.

The point is that from our earliest moments the authoritative voices leave their mark and can become the internalised taskmasters of adult life. Not to say that is always a bad thing, it is neither good nor bad, it is simply one manifestation of the mechanistic workings of survival mind. It appears that now you have a choice whether or not you consent to the authority of the old, familiar internal 'oughts' and 'shoulds', the expectations of yourself, all of which constitute, originally, someone else's idea of how you should live your life.

Also, arising from your sensitivity, which is taken as read by the mere fact that you are consulting this book, early experiences of the world outside yourself will have prompted decisions about your interaction with it and the people in it. Those decisions assume authority in your life and become more powerful by repetition, and by your consent. There are many of them, but a few examples could be 'I don't belong', 'I can't have what I want', 'I have to manage on my own', 'I have to be a certain way to be loved' and so on. You get the idea.

In a very practical way, people and situations may be arising right now that reflect these internalised authorities that you carry. Another opportunity to look in the mirror. Some of those old imprints are undoubtedly past their 'sell by' date. This may be the time therefore for you to make a conscious choice about the validity of your continuing consent.

If such consent is appropriate, and freely given, fine, that can be just as liberating as the other alternative, which is to withdraw your consent, to terminate your agreement with them, and thereby take back your power. Either way, the point is you have reached a time, and a place in you, where this whole issue is subject to your choice.

We do not become enlightened by imagining figures of light, but by making the darkness conscious

You are engaged in the quest for personal enlightenment, whatever that may mean to you. Liberation, transformation, enlightenment may be synonyms for the rewards you seek by travelling the so called spiritual path. Whenever you made the choice to make that journey, whatever your age or stage of life, the timing is always appropriate.

In the early days, the honeymoon period if you like, it is common to pursue new and exciting concepts and ideas, belief systems about the deeper questions which, at last, make some sense of it all. Invariably, this time, which can last a lifetime, is accompanied by many and varied positive symbols appearing in your life.

There is a delight in discussion and sharing with those of like mind, you may even feel evangelistic about your discoveries. In significant dreams or meditations you may have visions of beautiful light–filled situations or figures. Indeed, with visualisation techniques you could find yourself as part of an uplifting scenario and feeling pleased to be 'out of the body' for a while. The opening of doors within you can give rise to others noticing new and positive things about you. Sensitives may give you messages which are distinctly other worldly and which encourage you in your new direction. Your own intuition and imagination may be awakened and supported as never before. All of which is wonderful, desirable, and necessary to get you off and running. However, the sweetness and light you have encountered is only half the story, half of who you are, half of what you have to make friends with in yourself if you are to achieve your goal.

We are all light and shade. We are used to being categorised, being put into convenient boxes, we are this or we are that, the purpose of which is to make us easy and safe to handle and, ultimately, control. The truth is, at the personal level, we are all multi-faceted, and will respond or react differently depending on the area of life we are involved in at the time. For example, we might be peaceful and serene when with friends, and full of suppressed anger and/or grief in the family or in intimate relationship; happy at work and unhappy at home, and so on.

This text is to remind you that the sweetness and light on your path is valid and necessary to your impetus and that, of itself, it is unable to facilitate your liberation. You have reached the point at which you have to become familiar with your shadow. To bring what has been judged to be negative, or unwelcome, or just plain wrong, up to the surface, up to consciousness where it can be acknowledged, experienced, accepted and embraced as a valid part of you, as a friend. Otherwise your path to the mountaintop will be beset with a weight of baggage on your back which will become heavier and heavier until you grind to a halt.

To refer to the light and shade in you is a necessary acknowledgement of duality. However, how you hold that duality makes all the difference. When you view both impostors with no more favouritism than you would grant say one eye over the other, or one arm over the other, you know you've cracked it!

You can do anything, or go anywhere, if you're not in a hurry

Slow down buster! Could be there's something you want so badly, a goal you're working so hard to reach, and it doesn't seem to be getting any nearer. Could be your life is so full of things to do, duties, responsibilities, that you are always in a hurry. This text can be a simple reminder to be patient with yourself and with life, everything has its time, be it a vast project or a simple household chore. That can be infuriating, someone or something urging you to be patient, but this is one of those times when there is little choice. You will get what's coming to you exactly when you're supposed to, and not a moment sooner.

The origin of this saying came from the lips of a penniless beach bum who had been all over the world, often to places most others dream about, practising what he preached. He had learned the wisdom of the words in his travels, and was a deeply contented man.

Being in a hurry is a subjective state, and one that you can do something about. When you are travelling from point A to point B, by whatever means, and at whatever speed, you can do it in an internal state of 'hurry, hurry, hurry', or in a place of inner calm, knowing that you'll get there when you get there.

The analogy of the mythical race between the tortoise and the hare comes to mind. The tortoise goes at his own pace and defeats the hare, encumbered as he is with all his manic distractions along the way. You may be resembling the hare just now, with the imposition of anxiety and other internal pressures carried together with diverting interests erected en route to the desired goal.

How many times have you been driving to keep an appointment and, believing you are short of time, carried impatience and anxiety as extra baggage, only to encounter roads full of slow moving traffic ahead of you? When you're not in a hurry, no extra subjective baggage, lo and behold, the same roads are clear, or the traffic is moving quickly and easily.

In any case, trying to rush things, efforting to move fast, or faster than usual, often results in slip ups along the way, and by the time you've corrected those you have probably taken longer than you would by taking it calmly, easily, in the first place.

Don't get sucked into the form. You can cover the ground you have to cover at the same speed, get there at the same time, but your experience of the journey can be either 'in a hurry' or 'not in a hurry' – that part of it is up to you. Try it. Be at ease. Chill. You will always do precisely what you were meant to do, go exactly where you were meant to go, at the time intended – Big Daddy's got it all in hand!

Never underestimate the power of denial

Are you being denied, or are you doing the denying? Probably both, for if you are being denied something or someone in your outer world, then at some level you may have already said 'No thanks'. A sure sign of deeper denial is a repeating pattern of not getting what you want, perhaps in a specific area of your life. The object of your desire, be it a person or thing, is continually presented as unobtainable, and always for the best of reasons, apparently.

If this is the case, it may be time to look beyond your material efforts to attain the goal, and delve into other parts of the energy system which is you to see what is actually preventing attainment. If there is an early decision rooted in the sub-conscious which conflicts with the adult conscious desire, the latter doesn't stand a chance.

In any power struggle between the sub–conscious and the conscious, the sub-conscious always wins, which is, incidentally, why hypnotism works – the hypnotist knows how to bypass the conscious and put suggestions, i.e. new decisions, directly into the sub-conscious, thus the more spectacular stage demonstrations.

Examples? Imagine a young child who only receives the love and attention she craves when she is unwell. That could create an early decision attaching love and attention to illness. That experience and the decision resulting from it becomes enfolded in the sub-conscious as her conscious mind receives its conditioning cloak. Later, she longs for good health and well being, only to be beset by a long medical history. Even, possibly, when minor illnesses don't prompt care and attention, the afflictions will become more serious until the demands of that early decision are satisfied.

Imagine another young child who has a deep sense of betrayal early in life, perhaps through birth trauma or an experience of abandonment. That could produce an attachment of extreme pain to the mother's love, and thereby an early decision to keep that love and anything like it at a distance. By the time adulthood is reached, that decision is completely buried in the sub-conscious and dictates a barrier to intimacy with partners no matter what the power and needs of the conscious drive.

The point of all this is to illustrate that choosing this text may be directing you to look deeper within yourself for the causes and ultimate release of denial in your life. There are many ways of doing that. Choose the person and the technique carefully. The process of making the sub-conscious conscious is worthwhile, and, because deep feelings are usually involved, a safe environment is important, often, but not exclusively, the therapeutic one.

Equally, there may be someone near and dear to you who is clearly in denial about some aspect of themselves or their lives. You may have been trying to hold up a mirror for them, yet with the best of intentions on your part, the reflection is not seen. No one can do anything until the other is ready to look, and the timing of that is not up to you. In fact you can best serve them by letting go the effort.

The gift to yourself could be the emerging recognition that anything less than that which gives you the most joy is denial. Do what makes you fly – and you will have broken the power of denial.

Liberation for some requires that they be released from past vows

Attachments can take many forms. We can be attached to situations, material things, people; past, present, even future events, by our conditioning and by our hopes, plans, expectations. We can be attached physically, emotionally, mentally and spiritually, or any permutation of all of these. Of themselves they are neither good nor bad, they are simply necessary mechanisms for survival, until, of course, we move beyond survival to a fuller expression of life. Some of them we are quite happy to have and they serve as life enhancing. Most of us carry some attachments at any given time which may have been life enhancing once but now tend to hamper and restrict us in some way. This page reflects the presence of the latter, and in a particular form.

Vows taken to a cause, a relationship, a way of life, particularly in the midst of a ritual or ceremony, run very deeply in our consciousness. They can involve us at every level of our being, often more than we realise. The depth of commitment, where vows are involved, takes us to a place in ourselves which transcends the everyday promises and agreements we make, and so the strength of attachment is correspondingly greater.

This text is indicating that part of your consciousness is trying to tell you there are vows you made in the past which are still present within you, still pulling the strings of your life in some way, when their relevance no longer exists. An example of this may be marriage vows if the marriage is now past history. Attachment can still be in place to the former partner, or your way of life in partnership, or events and traumas within the marriage. If this has resonance within then it's time to consciously release yourself from those vows, there is need to be free of them.

For many who seek expansion and liberation from a restricted sense of self, these words may mean something deeper yet. It is possible that, in this life, or indeed a previous one if your belief system encompasses that, you have taken religious vows of some sort. A typical example would involve the severe restrictions imposed by the monastic life in our past history. Vows of this sort have included denial on a grand scale. Life had to be lived under strict disciplines which imposed poverty, chastity, and even silence in some cases.

The motivation was of the highest, and this is not a judgement of that way of life, past or present, but is intended as a timely prompt for a look at the denial in your life as you live it now. Feel if any of it may be related to a continuing attachment to old, old vows of this kind which are making an obsolete and negative contribution to the quality of your life now. If there is a resonance, again, it is time for conscious release of those vows on your part, and prayer and meditation requesting the granting of absolution from them by Divine Intelligence. It may help the process to write, and to say out loud as a mantra, the following words, or your own personal adaptation of them.

I, ... *full name* ... , ask to be released from all vows and commitments made by me, or any manifestation of my self, in this and any previous lifetimes, which have served their purpose and thus are detrimental to me and the quality of my life in this and any future lifetimes.

In the longest hours of darkness we birth our true beauty and love

Anything and everything worthy of manifestation requires a gestation period. A seed needs its time in the ground. Most evident to us is the mammalian requirement for adequate time in the womb. In any act of creation, be it through the medium of nature in all its wonders, or via the apparently more controlled channel of human creativity, the seed that has been sown has to be nurtured and given the right conditions to come to fruition in due time.

Those conditions, so necessary to creation in the form, can appear dark, oppressive, restricting, frightening even, and that may be how your life appears to you at the moment. The energy of this text is that of encouragement and support during this time, for there are parts of your being waiting to come into the light of day which require no reason, no rationale, they simply are parts of your humanity which have not yet had the chance to be seen and felt.

Don't try and work it out. Know that you are in a process of change and when the current darkness has passed you will never be quite the same again. Divine Intelligence is at work here. This is beyond your control. It is in the hands of the same Intelligence which makes your heart beat, your hair grow, your digestive system turn food into energy, your nervous system work like a vast Internet within your body, and all without any conscious intervention on your part.

Consider the creation of a butterfly – what a beautiful symbol of transformation! The seed, the pattern, the blueprint of the butterfly is present in the lowly caterpillar even while it is a worm crawling on its belly. As night follows day the beauty of the butterfly must manifest to enrich the environment. Whatever the risks it will emerge to fulfil its destiny. And yet. And yet. First the caterpillar must withdraw into its cocoon, become a chrysalis, endure the darkness, the mystery of transmutation, time must pass in this state for the miracle to happen.

This is where you are. You don't know the depth of the beauty and love within you. Let the mystery remain, don't intervene. That would be like opening up the chrysalis prematurely to see if the butterfly is there yet. Your mind may be attached to the current darkness as a negative state, that is understandable.

However, this is a reminder that something else is going on, parts of you are to be revealed which will far outweigh the apparent negativity of the present time. That revelation is worth waiting for; it is worth the long hours of darkness. The light of day unfailingly follows the night..

In the process of life itself

As never before, now is a time of surfacing imbalances. Opening the book here could mean you are facing an upwelling of unfamiliar feelings, attitudes, judgements – particularly of yourself – and personal challenges on an unprecedented level. With the rational analysis that you are likely to apply to try and sort it all out, you're not going to get very far, because what is going on, or rather coming up for attention, is likely to be surfacing from the irrational, sub-conscious part of you.

Any apparent ease in life is but a veneer whilst we are still at the mercy of surface conditions. When even that fragile state disappears, we are literally in a state of dis-ease; disease at any or all levels makes its presence felt, physically, emotionally and mentally. What is happening now could be viewed as a necessary revealing of the underbelly of your life. Anything formerly repressed, avoided, denied or hidden about yourself is trying to reach the light, like a germinating seed finding a way for its shoots to appear above the surface of the earth and overcoming all obstacles to it doing so.

It would be understandable to regard current conditions as negative, perhaps in the extreme, or a temporary blip to be overcome, to be confronted, fought or put in their place; the martial language emerges. At one level, compared with your previous state, negativity seems to hold sway.

However, there is another view and, no, this is not a plug for positive thinking and other current obsessions with trying to apply the conscious mind to what is essentially unconscious in origin. What is being presented is another opportunity to embrace the whole of your humanity rather than just the previously acceptable part of it. There is material here that is being externalised, as it must, and former mindsets, belief systems and methodologies simply will not work. A shift is being demanded and here's a paradox; it's nothing to do with you personally.

We are living in a time when the hidden must be revealed; this is happening individually and universally. There is a shift taking place and it's huge. The energy field in which we all live and move and have our being, is on the move; it is a time of transition and the signs are present constantly. Life is always trying to restore balance, to the macrocosm and the microcosm. Just as storms can be simple adjustments to extremes of air pressure in proximity, thus apparent negative states in us, particularly the unfamiliar ones, are sure signs of the presence of imbalances demanding to be included in the process of life itself.

The message here is important to you at this time as never before. Whatever is happening within and without is bound to occur. The unmanifest has to become manifest, so do not hold it all as some kind of comment on you personally; be aware that the self-valuations and judgements that your mind may be all too ready to produce are not valid. The basis of your life is having a clear-out!

The basement and the attic have to be cleared in the process of the move within and without. Run with it, allow it its life. Whether or not they realise it, this process is coming up for everyone and at every level of every society. Awareness is the key to holding it all in the crucible of your inward ease. Remember, the only constant in life is change – a cliché maybe, but true nevertheless.

When you have peace
you have everything

The capacity for peace exists within all of us, and yet, when pressed, many people, when asked what they want most in life, in other words what they are missing most, will have an answer which includes the word peace. 'To find some peace', 'Be at peace with myself', 'Peace of mind', 'World peace', and so on; that's normally after a list of material additions desired first of course. Peace in some form is pretty near bedrock for many of us, and by defining what we want we confirm that we haven't got it now!

Peace has become like a commodity which, until we learn otherwise, is pursued by the attempt to build material buttressing. So we try and achieve an inner state by the acquisition and control of outer circumstances. It is absolutely legitimate to try and create material stability and well being for ourselves, those dear to us, and ultimately the wider community.

That quest could also be called the search for security and is, more often than not, measured by reference to our relationships with the contents of our outer life. As the latter is always changing, so called security is a myth. If all the conditions for security were fulfilled we wouldn't move an inch outside our front door, or even out of the favourite chair. Yet comfort, safety, stability are held by the conditioned mind to be routes to peace. There can be none whilst we persist in our search on such shifting sands.

The language used here is that of possession – 'When you *have* peace, you *have* everything.' Whatever your outer conditions, you can have peace within – it is yours already, and your capacity for it is about to be revealed. It is a state which exists regardless of judgement of your material life. Which would you rather be, a rich, successful figure in constant inner turmoil, or a humble roadsweeper at peace with him/herself? Did I hear you say 'No contest!'

The conditioned mindset demands that we have reasons to be happy, or at peace. Not so. You can realise an inner state by going within and being unreasonable. Try it – spend a minute, an hour, a day, being at peace for no reason, you don't need reasons. Your capacity for this state may blink when first allowed into the light of day, but it will grow used to it with practice.

Remember, having that inner peace doesn't mean you don't do anything. It does not depend on sitting quietly in a darkened room listening to your favourite soothing music, nice though that can be. You will recognise it by its presence even in the midst of doing, in the midst of activity. You will recognise it by an overwhelming sense that everything is exactly as it should be, in the moment. The constant desire for some aspect of your life to be other than it is will drop away. Everything is perfectly alright precisely the way it is, right now. You have everything; you want for nothing.

By the way, don't beat yourself up when you lose it, peace is always available to you whenever you are prepared to be unreasonable. It is not called the peace that 'passeth all understanding' for nothing!

The quickest way to end a miracle is to ask it why it is or what it was

To have a text to back up this aphorism seems to fly in the face of the essential energy reflected here. On the other hand there might be a miracle occurring in your life at this time and you need some help to recognise its presence.

Miracles take on many guises. One definition could be the manipulation of time and space in a way that transcends natural law, or the current understanding of what constitutes natural law. (Today's miracles are tomorrow's science). Water into wine, raising the dead would qualify. Throughout history masters and avatars have demonstrated their mastery of energy management in this way. Instantaneous healing of a deadly disease was certainly regarded as a miracle, now such a description would be regarded with suspicion and disbelief, except of course by the recipient in any age.

Therein lies the rub. It depends on your stance, your mindset, as to what is miraculous and what is not. For some that which is beyond reason would be a miracle, or, at least, feel like one. You may have been facing what appeared to be an insurmountable obstacle in some area of your life and then, suddenly, for no apparent reason, the obstacle fades away and you move on. Fine, the message here is, don't try and figure it out, just rejoice, be grateful, accept the miraculous gift.

You may have emerged from a period of darkness, of negativity, without any effort on your part. It suddenly clears and you feel lighter, life is brighter. Great! Don't bother to question it. The part of you that always wants to question, to ask 'Why?' or 'What?' is the mechanism which will close the door on the wonder of the experience. This is a time to say to your rational mind 'No, I'm not interested in the reasons, go attach yourself to something else in my life where reasoning is more appropriate right now.' Just as you might refuse demands for yet another chocolate bar from an errant child.

Then there are the ordinary everyday miracles which we take for granted. On a sunny day the sky is blue instead of the black of space. We can explain it, but why bother, why not just enjoy it. We can take a childlike delight in the evidence all around us of the maintenance and growth of anything and everything organic, including ourselves. It all happens by never ending simple cell division – ain't that a miracle?!

Take your pick as to which of these miracles is present in your life now. Be assured it is a miraculous time for you, and whatever qualifies, throw your arms around it as if it were a huge bouquet of flowers. When you receive flowers you don't ask where, how, or why the flowers grew do you?!

You have to give up the life you planned for the life that's waiting for you

This text has several implications. It's about the place of planning in your life. It's about recognising there is a greater plan than yours in operation. It's about the interplay between times of being fixed and inflexible, and times of flexibility and going with the flow. It's about being able to change your mind and your direction spontaneously. It's about courage.

You may have a good idea of where your life is going on several fronts, or at least where you want it to go. You may even have written down detailed specifications of your future requirements at many levels of your being and doing in this world. Have you noticed that sometimes this seems to work and sometimes it doesn't, so it is not a method to be relied on, there must be some other principle at work here. That principle has been defined in many ways in many apparently differing religions, philosophies, belief systems.

It could be said that when your conscious desires are in line with the 'Divine Plan' they will come to fruition, when they're not, they won't. What does 'Fate' have in store for you? Eastern philosophies speak to us of the 'Akashic Record' which represents the whole of human history already in place, like an eternal symphony with every note composed, and we're all simply following our music sheets.

There's nothing wrong with planning. It has its place, even if only to still the mind or subvert confusion – just don't get attached to the results that's all, they may not be in line with the tune you're here to play.

If you've opened the book here, it's an indication that life may be presenting ways of changing direction in a significant part of your life. Situations and people may be coming your way bringing opportunities in many disguises. They can be obvious or subtle. Heighten your awareness of what comes in to your environment which is exciting, challenging, stimulating, threatening even. The potential will certainly be present for you to behave in a way which is not your norm.

Above all be prepared to be flexible. Rigid adherence to your plans, great or small, is not the best way right now. Give yourself permission to change your plan, even throw it out of the window. It is always your prerogative to change your mind if you choose. You may upset those around you who depend on a certain perception of you for their own stability, their own security, this is not a time to let such dependence rule your actions. This is a time for you to take what may feel like a risky course, to have the courage to abandon a plan or plans and play the music it was always intended you should play.

By the way, don't beat yourself up if you see such opportunities only in hindsight to begin with, Divine Intelligence knows better than you how long it will take to get through to the required response.

Keep your options open

It is likely that you are faced with what feels like an important decision. To decide involves the killing of alternatives. The words ending in ...cide indicate that there is the prospect of a death of some kind; suicide – death of the self; fratricide – death of a brother; genocide – the killing of a whole nation or ethnic group; and so on. It appears that a time of decision is upon you.

Not so. In the pressing matter before you, the pressure to decide, to kill the alternatives, may be coming from within, and be a product of your own conditioning, or from without, with people and situations apparently demanding that you be decisive. On the contrary, right now your best course is to allow the alternatives before you to live, for a while longer at least.

Timing is critical, and just as there is an optimum time for decision, there is also a time for allowing that moment to arrive, and you are currently in the latter. For now, the effluxion of time will reveal the most desirable direction, and such revelation can not be forced. Indeed, to do so might well prove counter productive in the long run.

You are faced with the difference between the survival drives of surface mind, and the greater wisdom of the process of life itself, which, if allowed to flow without the compulsive interventions of the former, always brings healing to the fore represented in this case by the resolution likely for the highest good.

What is also possible here is that the alternatives presented seem to be of equal validity. There is no obvious choice. The good news is that you can't make a mistake, there is no 'right' or 'wrong' road to take, either will take you where you need to go.

We live in a world in which duality is inherent, some of which we accept and take for granted, e.g. up/down, day/night, male/female, and so on, but most of which we hold as something to be resolved one way or another, a problem to be solved. What then is normal and co-existing in twoness becomes subject to judgement, the cementing of a mindset in the correctness, the 'truth' of one of the alternatives. Two aspects of almost anything in human affairs are labelled typically 'right' and 'wrong'. The surface mind is programmed to choose one over the other and then, tragically, identify with it.

What may be prevalent with you is the need to embrace paradox, that both sides or even all sides of the equation you are facing are equally valid – there is more than one 'right' way – and what is required is not a decision, there is no need to kill the alternatives, just proceed down one path knowing that the others remain open to you if needed. Human law is a function of duality; Divine law is a function of unity.

The brighter the light, the darker the shadow

This is a reminder of the essential duality of life, particularly evident at the personal level. Imagine being outside on a bright sunny day. Wherever you go, whatever you do, you will cast a shadow in the opposite direction to that from which the light comes. Bearing in mind the old adage 'As above, so below', the physical presence of light and shade symbolises a duality which exists at other levels of experience, in particular the realms of thought and emotion.

Even as a simple analogy this text works as an illustration of the fluctuations of human personality. Think of the bright lights shed on every aspect of society by those with creative, innovative, or artistic genius, and how often that is accompanied by a personal darkness every bit as intense as the light they give out. Mozart and Van Gogh come to mind.

What does all this mean for you? Choosing this page, you are probably feeling very bright or very dark right now. Whichever it is, don't be attached to it. If life is light and you are currently in good space, trying to hold on to it will merely speed its departure. If life seems black at the moment, allow it to be that way and it will pass. Resisting it, trying to 'make it right', fighting it, will keep it hanging around – what you resist, persists.

This is a reminder that life is cyclic. The dark and the light will come and go. The cycle of night and day every 24 hours doesn't present any problems, we take it for granted. So it is with our inheritance of personality on this planet.

If you are in the light half of the equation currently, be sure to enjoy it for what it is. Trying to work it out, looking for reasons for it so you can repeat it to order will move you into the shade quicker than necessary. Being in that bright place means that, for a while, there is space in the energy system which is you, there is an alignment in the pipework which allows easy flow.

What happens then? There is room for more of what needs to be cleared to come through and occupy that space, more of the shadow which needs to be acknowledged and experienced so that the purpose of the cycle is fulfilled, namely the restoration of balance. Healing in the very process of life itself. All we have to do is get out of the way!

If you are in a dark place, two things. One, this too shall pass. Two, in a strange way be encouraged, for this text emphasises that whatever the intensity of the darkness you are feeling, you must therefore be capable of a similar intensity of brightness, it is within you awaiting its cyclic rebirth.

Let it flow and let it go

Only seven words and yet here is the key to emotional good health. It is likely that there is an emotion, or a whole bag of them, making their presence felt in your life at this time, and this text highlights the need to simply feel them without blocking or denying them, and then let them go without prolonging attachment to them, or judgement of yourself for having them.

It is no accident that we use the language of fluidity and the emotions together. We talk of being calm and calm waters, of tears flowing, of angry seas, of raging waters, of a gushing personality, and so on. In esoteric writings water is a symbol of the emotions. Water in all its forms can be life giving or life destroying, just as our emotional life and our reaction to it can be creative or destructive of our health and well being.

The point is, water and the emotions share this simple truth of their existence, they both seek the line of least resistance and flow along it. That is all our feelings ever want to do. The problems start when we believe that any emotion is intrinsically 'wrong', or there must be something wrong with us for having it. Having feelings is not a problem until and unless we make it into one with the machinery of judgement and control which is present in our conditioned thinking.

Judging some emotions as right and others as wrong, or some positive and others negative, interferes with the flow of feelings – and that's all they want to do, flow through our consciousness just like a river flowing through a landscape which is the richer for it being there. When the river is not allowed to flow it will damage that landscape instead of fructifying and supporting it.

What constricts or blocks the flow typically is the thought that certain of our emotions are aberrations and have to be 'healed'. No, the blockage is the problem, not the emotion. Joy, sadness, bliss, fear, love, anger, rage, grief, ecstasy, lust, compassion, and on and on – all of them simply energy in motion – e-motion. Another way of expressing the wisdom of this saying is to acknowledge the feeling currently demanding attention, allow it its life, and let it flow on through without judgement or attachment. That way you will emerge the better for the experience rather than feeling damaged by it.

One thing to be aware of – to 'beware' of – allowing an emotion its life, allowing it to flow through your being, does not necessarily mean it has to be acted out in the world. Acknowledging the truth of its existence in yourself, recognising it for what it is – a personally felt energy wanting to move through you – is often enough to let it go on its way; the tide ebbs. (Isn't it interesting how often we hear the phrase 'I was moved' as an expression of a recognised emotion within.).

Observing your internal reality in this way is powerful. However, sometimes the intensity of the emotion felt demands that it be expressed in the form of acting it out, in the form of catharsis of some sort. That has to be recognised too, and, in its turn, demands that you find a safe time and place for that cathartic reaction.

Understanding? I've understood all my life and not lived a minute! Now my minute is almost gone

This is yet another cry from the heart to be let out from under the burden of an ever hungry intellectual need. Look at the word understanding – what is it you are standing under?! If you have chosen this text it is telling you that it is time to emerge from the tyranny imposed by the controlling mind's never ending question 'Why?' and start to live a little, a lot in fact. Incidentally, have you noticed how an answer to the question 'Why?' usually leads to another 'Why?' and on and on.

Let's be clear, there's nothing wrong with understanding, basically it means embracing an explanation which we find satisfactory, for a time at least. In this context however, it is only satisfying to the intellect, and the value of that part of our functioning has been vastly over inflated for decades, if not centuries, to the detriment of a fuller expression of who we are. We may have the material results of the burgeoning intellect and call it progress, but is there any evidence to suggest that we are any happier, or more at peace with ourselves because of it?

Right there is the question you may have been asking yourself recently, and the answer may have been something similar to the essence of this text. You may have a wealth of understanding about yourself, about life, even about the deepest philosophical questions and still be living a life which is half a life, or no life at all.

This is a wake up call. Before it's too late, move beyond the observation, the understanding, the control, and jump! Feel the sensual longings of your body for movement, for touch, taste, smell, sight, hearing and do something about them. Be aware of each sense functioning for its own sake, not just for survival, or for a result, but for the joy of having that sense awake and alive in you.

Allow yourself to feel your emotions doing their best to enrich your life – for heaven's sake don't try and work them out, just let them flow. Emotions couldn't care less about being understood, or rationalised, they just want to be felt so they can flow on through the energy system which is you. Listen to your imagination, your intuition, your creativity, let yourself daydream once in a while.

Many rewarding experiences are judged to be escapism and thus discarded; don't you believe it, that's just the time when inspiration and guidance can find a way in. There's so much more to being human than mere understanding.

You're still in the body, so it's not too late. Understanding is the booby prize, the bottom rung on the ladder of true self discovery. So don't stand under the ladder any longer, move on up past the demands of intellect to the riches beyond.

We must be betrayed

In all our attempts to relate to one another, probably the two most common and most hurtful and deeply felt estrangements are separation and betrayal. They always seem to arise in direct proportion to the depth of love and vulnerability we have allowed ourselves to feel toward another, usually in close intimate relationship, but not exclusively. Any relationship where there has been a measure of the three biggies – honesty, safety, and commitment – can qualify.

Our ability to suffer the pangs of betrayal, and our reaction to them, can not arise unless there is a form of love present. If our feelings are not objectified, then we are indifferent, and betrayal does not arise. So, it appears that a loved one, in whatever role in your life, has let you down. The first thing to be aware of is that might actually be true, or simply appear to be that way. Betrayal is so much part of our psychology that we tend to see it all too readily in the words, actions and body language of the beloved other when the betrayal is 'in the eye of the beholder'. Communicate and do your best to establish the reality; you may be hurting unduly. The beloved may be truly innocent and your feelings the result of your projection.

Another possibility, and by far the most usual provocation of feelings of betrayal, is the direction of affections away from you. Again, apparent or actual, the pain is just as intense. The variations on this theme are endless. Someone else, or something else, or simple withdrawal and unavailability now dominate the emotional territory you regarded as your own. Even the death of the beloved can be held as a form of betrayal: 'How dare you leave me!'

Whatever it is and however it has arisen, it is here, now. Time to have your feelings whatever they are. What is happening defies denial, avoidance or burial. Sadness, grief, anger, rage even – they are all valid. Don't let anybody tell you to 'snap out of it.' The first inclination is to direct all the hurt at the beloved other. The blame game is recognised, but still supported and perpetuated throughout society. You may need to go through that initially, but don't get stuck in it as so many do, for then it can go on forever. See it as part of the process of healing the wound.

Sooner or later you get to the 'Why me?' stage. This may be where you are now. That is to be applauded, because it means you are starting to look inwardly rather than projecting it all on to an outward source. Betrayal is built into the human condition; we will always attract it one way or another so long as we depend on anyone else to provide a measure of who and what we are. When the pain has served its purpose, we can give in to being human. We can start to accept that we are absolutely fine and how we are meant to be, warts and all, regardless of what anyone or anything else manifests around us.

There is a knowing that whatever life presents, we are a suitable conduit for it to flow through. If you are not already there, you are certainly on the brink of this profound state. Apparent betrayal in the world as it is will always be a presence; however, your attachment to it is about to change, and letting that go is the ultimate healing of all wounds.

They change their climate, not their lives, who rush across the sea

One of the most seductive illusions we can hold is the one that says if we change some part of our material reality our lives will change for the better. It is easy to believe that if we alter some aspect of the mundane, the outer life, then the inner life must follow. All the 'if only' statements apply. 'If only I had a new relationship/house/job/car everything would be alright, I would be fine.'

Sooner or later we discover that such motivation is bound to fail. The new acquisition or change of circumstances may well bring a temporary boost in energy or self esteem. Then, all too quickly such results can fade into the background of the reality we were trying to change, and the latter re-asserts itself. The familiar behaviour patterns, energy levels, decisions and judgements about ourselves and about life, all tend to reappear.

This is a reminder to you not to be deluded by the mindset so described at this time. You may be considering a move, perhaps as big as emigration, or at least time away from your own culture, your own homeland, all in the interests of changing your life at depth. It's not about warning you off such a move. It may well be a great adventure at one level.

The whole point of this page is to make you aware that, of itself, a material change alone will not achieve what you are really looking for, the focus of your heart's yearnings. Changing your surroundings for the new and unfamiliar may well be appealing.

However, for the moment, the rewards you really seek are more likely to be found right under your nose.

The real source of any profound move does not come from outside to in. You are still the same you in whatever corner of the globe appears to have the answers. The flow of energy which will make a difference is the other way around, from inside to the outer world. When the shift has taken place within, then it will bring about whatever new circumstances such a shift demands. It must happen that way – it's simply the way the fountain of life's energies work.

We are still conditioned to believe that the outer manipulates the inner – that can appear to be true in the short term, but what you are looking for requires the long term answer. The big moves can and do correspond with shifts taking place or already achieved inwardly. Then what is experienced is more than just a change of climate, indeed it is more likely to transcend change altogether, it becomes transformation.

The energy around you is stressing that this is not a time to rush into significant moves. Wait for those shifts in you which will take place, given time, then make your move, and rejoice in changing much more than just the climate!

If you want to still the mind
– move the body

The mind at its most intrusive is a thought producing machine. The part of it which is conditioned for our survival in the world continually converts life force into a stream of concepts, ideas, rationalisations, judgements, projections, and what we think of as reality checks. It is never off duty. It is the hamster in the wheel.

Some eastern spiritual traditions regard the mind as the insane monkey inside us all. The trouble is it is very easy to fall into a life pattern of racing along behind the monkey attempting to follow its dictates and directions and always falling short – there's another judgement!

One of the most common answers to the question 'What do you want most in life?' is 'Peace of mind'. A huge step toward that goal is to be at peace with the mind exactly as it is in any given moment. That requires detachment in the sense of moving away from total identification with the thought machine. Taking a step back and watching the machinery working, observing your thoughts instead of thinking you *are* them. Millions of words over hundreds of years have been written about myriad ways of achieving inner peace which is needed now more than ever.

The key to give you an appreciation of this energy is one of the simplest in the human condition, and yet it is rarely appreciated, namely that the mind excels in keeping you in the past or the future, whereas the body is always in the present. The most effective meditation techniques make use of this by bringing attention to the body and the senses initially, and soon the initiate notices that the insane monkey gradually slows down.

Opening the book here is putting you on notice to take another route into the body. You can slow down the thought processes, even experience windows of stillness, times of no thought, of relative peace, by giving your body something to do. The monkey stops chattering, takes a break from its crazy antics.

This is a time to 'get out of your head' and into your body. Any activity which calls for movement of your body is going to be of benefit at this time, and the more physical you can be the better. Exercise as vigorously as you can, dance, move to some music which really grabs you, walk fast, jog, run, swim, cycle – whatever your thing is, do it! Vacuum the house, clean the car, cut the grass, but at twice the usual speed! You get the idea.

Your mind may attempt to defend its dominance and produce thoughts like 'I don't feel like it' or 'This is silly, how can this still my mind?' It can even fill your day with all kinds of compulsions so 'I don't have time for this' comes up. It is a very clever monkey. If you're reading this text, trust the energy it is reflecting to you and *move*!

Don't get involved in the problem – put your energy into observing it, be a witness to its passing

What are you caught up in? There is something going on in your life right now which is dominating your thoughts and feelings to such an extent that you feel ineffective even at the simplest of everyday tasks. It could be that you've had some kind of confrontation and felt that you came off worst because you didn't say what you wanted to say, the right words came to mind too late.

Maybe a confrontation with a particular person is needed and you're avoiding it. You could be in a job or career which you hate, or at least doesn't serve you any more. There could be a home or family situation which has become intolerable. How about relationship? Perhaps you're in one and you want to be out of it; or you are without one and you want one. Whatever it is, your involvement in it is controlling you, dictating your current quality of life.

Another way of describing this energy is that it denotes the giving away of personal power. All your energy is being sucked into the problem – thinking about it, worrying about it, trying to work it out – all draining you, leaving you tired. In extremis even depressed or despairing.

The greatest problem in any apparently negative situation is not in the objective world but in the subjective one. For example, it may be natural to feel impatient for the cloud or clouds to pass, but this is not the time to let your actions or even your attitude to the problem be driven by impatience.

Equally plausible would be an attachment to solving the problem as quickly as possible, when it might be appropriate, particularly as you have opened the book here, to take a step back and let life take its course. Just watch what happens, it might surprise you.

It is time to take your power back. Withdraw your attention from the problem back to the present moment. If there is something you can do about it right now – do it! If not, let it go, you have no control in this moment. Then do whatever works for you to bring you back to a point of stillness within – it could be meditation, yoga, heavy exercise, a hot bath, sharing honestly with a trusted friend, there will be something which does it for you.

From that point of stillness, activate observation of the problem, just watch what's going on, without judgement of yourself or anyone else, be the witness – *being* the witness is a state of consciousness, it's not *doing* anything.

It doesn't mean you are not involved in the outer levels of living through the beginning, middle and ending of the problem, you will still go through the motions of it all. The difference is the experience becomes more like watching yourself act out a role in a play, you say the words, you go through the actions, and in the midst of it all there is a kernel of stillness, of knowing that 'this too shall pass'.

Everything has to go until there's nothing left

The wording sounds like a slogan painted across the shop window of a business closing down. In a sense that is true. Every 'thing' that has served its purpose has to go. No, it doesn't mean we have to give away everything we own, live a life free of material possessions and walk thereafter in poverty. That is not how it works. How many times do we have to be told, by the greatest teachers over the ages in various ways that 'the kingdom of heaven is within'. The material things may go or stay, that's not the point, it is our *attachment* to them as a measure of who and what we are which has to fall away.

The more profound message of this simple text concerns our inner world, for that is also full of things, stuff to which we are attached. If you're human and on the planet at this time there is likely to be a wealth of material in your inner life which you have carried around like a labouring ant with a load many times its own body weight. You may have become so used to the presence of that load that you don't even know it's there, unless, of course, you have embarked already on the mission of becoming aware of the content of your energy system and its place in dictating the quality of life you enjoy, or endure.

Whatever the content of the unfinished business you may be carrying around, now is the time you will be reminded of it. Wherever or whenever there has been an issue, a problem, an event, a person, normally involving trauma and pain at some level, and you are still attached because you didn't speak your truth or allow your true feelings their lives at the time, now is the time they will re-appear in some form.

Just remember the effluxion of time has no bearing on the intensity of the attachment – the origin of it could have been last week, or decades ago, psychologically we have the capacity to lug these things around for as long as it takes. Life will mirror them continually in people and events around you in everyday situations until you get the message, and getting it sufficiently to enable you to let go involves much more than the intellect.

Conscious recognition and acknowledgement are the first to arrive. Then understanding. Allowing the emotions their lives comes next, followed by some form of expression. Integration, and finally forgiveness, which cannot be forced, it will come as an holistic experience as a finale to the process.

Time is the great impostor. The whole process of becoming free of any attachment can take years, or moments. The evidence is that once the first step of acknowledgement has taken place the process is getting faster and faster, until we realise we're not doing it anyway, it is simply happening. We just witness it, watching transformation of our inner reality and its outer form, all of which is aided enormously by our giving up trying to control it.

Finally, the more 'somethings' we let go the less there is to define us, and the faster they appear for clearance until there's nothing left, there's no one there, there's *no thing* left. The attachments to the personality and the survival of the ego lose their significance.

Then we will truly be living in the world but not of it. That is the stuff of liberation, and you could be on the brink.

What you seek cannot be sought by conscious attention, only given. So stop seeking and receive

So much of our conditioning, particularly in the Western world, is geared toward achieving, toward the creating and attaining of goals, toward the merit in the effort required to bring them about. There is an obsession with growth, economically and personally, with 'bettering' ourselves, with acquisition of things taken as a measure of who we are.

There is always another place, another state of mind, which appears more desirable than exactly where we are, and off we go again on another treadmill. It matters not if you rebel, and try and get off the treadmill, the strength of the reaction, or the intensity of acquiescence, still indicate the power the conditioning has over you.

Awareness of the need to reach beyond conditioning may have dawned at some point, or simply the recognition that the material world and its apparent prizes are not the key to the peace you sought. These drives still emerge even when transferred to personal and spiritual 'development'.

Going deeply into that world what do we find? That all that drive to achieve has simply changed vehicles, only now all the books, lectures, courses, groups and so on are all about working toward different goals – changing your life for the better, change your mind and you will change your life, do this that or the other to be on your spiritual path, to access your higher self, whatever.

The underlying drive is still there, that there is somewhere to go, some goal to be achieved whatever the semantics. It can all be viewed as an attachment to doing as a means to attain a state of being, which is impossible whilst there is still attachment to the imagined goal. In other words whilst you are still seeking, still looking to go somewhere, to be on a journey, the very seeking ensures that the ineffable peace with yourself and with life remains just beyond reach.

To return to the wording of our heading, it could be said that conscious attention is itself a distraction from what you seek. Nothing wrong with conscious attention – it lends energy to any given goal, to any project, to any desire, giving a greater chance of its achievement. However, opening the book here is meant to show you that what you really desire, beyond all 'normal' earthly success in any given direction, is 'the peace that passeth all understanding'; not even a light bulb moment of enlightenment thank you, but the steady state of being which is your true legacy.

That is what is referred to here, and in that context, the mechanisms of conscious attention, which may bring you many things, but what you seek is essentially no-thing, nothing, and that is granted to you, it is not worked for, it cannot be sought with any hope of success. Divine Law is not to be confused with human law – 'My Ways Are Not Your Ways' – in other words I am mysterious – live with it, and see what comes your way.

Abolish the need to accomplish something and you clear the space in your energy field for the Infinite to enter. In terms of your deep spiritual need, there is nothing to accomplish; you are already all you need to be. So relax, let go, and receive. Say 'Yes' to love. Open your arms to love. Rest from seeking. It's all love anyway.

It is the season of silence and wonder; a time for the wisdom of inaction

Such a time is in the natural order of things, it's called Autumn. The progression of the seasons has reached its end. 'Now is the Winter of our discontent' conveys a clear meaning, except that the season is wrong. Autumn is the time of inevitable endings, closures, completions. More people depart this life in Autumn than in any other season, by far. Winter, not Spring, is the time for new beginnings, rebirth – life renews its form in Winter, but simply keeps it under wraps for the time being. The renewal becomes evident in Spring, when what was reborn out of sight emerges into the light of day.

So, now is the Autumn of your discontent. Nothing wrong with discontent, it can be a great driver to get things done when they need action. Yet, as always in the duality of the human condition, both action and inaction have their parts to play, and for the moment, the latter holds sway. The insane monkey in your head will always demand action, it is the ultimate control freak within all of us, particularly in western culture. Our conditioning is to act, to do, do, do. Well, now is a time to be, be, be.

Just imagine that the monkey is sated – well fed and dozy, he'll have his time again. Right now silence and wonder are the order of the day. You will still do what needs to be done to survive, but such doing is not where your greatest rewards are at this time. Intuition, inspiration, simply knowing when you don't know from whence they come, are the rewards on offer.

The busy-ness gets in the way usually, and the knowing that does make its presence felt has to squeeze in through cracks in the floorboards of the structure you call your life. How much easier it is to give the natural knowing in your heart, in every cell of your body, the chance to emerge into consciousness, by allowing periods of silence and wonder to take over, now more than ever.

As a potent symbol of what is appropriate, think of a landscape covered in snow. That has a silence all its own, and is a wonder to behold in its conversion of familiar objects, flora and fauna, to things of beauty not to be observed in quite the same way at any other time. That is where you are now. Contemplate every area of your life and, even if only for a short time every day, observe them in silence and wonder. Look at your particular garden of Eden in that state, and let the chattering monkey prattle on, as it will, with never ending judgements and instructions about what needs doing. If need be, get away from the clutter you are always attempting to deal with, or change, or improve, by reverting to Nature.

Right now there are huge benefits for you in this reminder, written by Lord Byron.

There is a pleasure in the pathless woods;
There is a rapture on the lonely shore;
There is society, where none intrudes,
By the deep sea, and music in its roar.
I love not man the less, but Nature more...

Should you be interested in a meeting for discussion about
this work, or any part of it, please email

r.alanhaven@btinternet.com

or

tambarnes@hotmail.co.uk